THE CYBER PATH

The infrastructure supporting the
Internet data flow

By

Lou Giannelli

To Cara, the ever present muse in my mind...

.,. per che tu sei incancellabile

Table of Contents

To order additional copies of this book, contact:
Xlibris
1-888-795-4274
www.Xlibris.com
Orders@Xlibris.com
791880

Preface

Journeying the cyber path is not a walk in the park. It is an odyssean experience, that one should be fully prepare to confront.

For the legendary hero in Greek mythology, Odysseus, it took 10 years to return home after the end of the Trojan War. Odysseus, the king of Ithaca, is portrayed in the Homeric epic "The Odyssey," in Books VI through XIII. According to Homer's account, the journey of Odysseus back to Ithaca is filled with adventurous and hazardous events, encountering a series of numerous dramatic circumstances and challenges between Troy and Ithaca. Every step of the way Odysseus encountered tests and battles, before being able to set foot back to Ithaca's soil.

When traversing the numerous cyber paths between source and destination, your binary data will also encounter an odyssean experience, and the digital data's owner will face many tests and battles as well. Just like in the Odyssey, many will try to capture, transform, steal, divert, and harm your data. In our times, information has becomes one of the most valuable commodities. And now that we have managed to manipulate and disseminate our information in digital format, the digital paths are assaulted by many threats and dangers created by those who seek to profit form our information.

This book will disclose to the reader a variety of cyber paths that are exposed to this odyssean experience. This book will also offer the reader with insight on some indicators on how to identify the presence of cyber threats, thus creating cyber awareness, and hopefully, encouraging the reader on how to take defensive measures, whenever such measures are feasible.

The primary goal of this book is to assist the reader in monitoring the correct cyber path that one's data should follow, and being able to detect when one's data may follow the incorrect path designed by malicious entities, seeking to harm the confidentiality, integrity, and availability of one's data.

Introduction

While using our cyber device of choice (desktop, laptop, tablet, smart phone, etc), do we ever have a conscious thought about the path that the cyber data we are processing in our device has followed, or will follow, from original source to final destination? Do we have a degree of awareness regarding the nature and composition of the infrastructure supporting the Internet data traffic flow?

This book will provide the reader with a broad scope of information regarding the amazing infrastructure supporting the Internet data flow. Why? Do we really care about knowing about this matter? We should, since having awareness of the intricate and complex path the cyber data flow traverses, and the accompanying threats at every step of the way, will give us a new insight into this process, and a new awareness regarding the corresponding threats affecting our cyber data, either at the personal or enterprise level.

This sense of awareness may lead us into an enhanced sense of responsibility to safeguard our data, and a rewarding sense of ownership and control in protecting the safety and integrity of the data we process in our cyber devices. The data set residing in our cyber devices may simply represent items of personal interest, but because it's our data set, speaks volumes regarding our personal identity and idiosyncrasies. Conversely, our data set may also contain confidential or sensitive information, or both.

The security of our data set, therefore, should be at the forefront of our priorities, simply because that data resides on cyber storage devices that may, at any given time, become discoverable by entities who may desire to exploit the contents of our data set for their own gain, to the detriment of our personal and family safety. Therefore, being aware of the path our data set travels is a constant priority; our identity and our personal interests and well being are at stake when we allow the proper attention due to this priority to decline.

Through the pages of this book we will travel many roads following different paths in our quest to gain the proper awareness we should all have regarding the cyber path of our data set. This awareness will provide you with a higher level of control and peace of mind in protecting your data set from prying eyes and malicious exploits. This journey will take you, in some cases, to roads you never knew existed, and threats you might have been, until now, completely incognizant.

Chapter 1. The Translator

This may not come as a surprise to many of the readers of this book, but we have to explicitly state it for the record: humans do not communicate in binary language, and electronic computers do not communicate in any human language; they only "speak" binary language (also known as "machine language").

So, it's obvious we are at an impasse. How do humans communicate with an electronic computer? Enter the keyboard, one of the most often used input devices assisting humans in interacting with electronic computers. It is thanks to this device, most of the time underestimated and taken for granted, that we humans can efficiently communicate with the binary device. We will briefly address the input/output (I/O) process model in some upcoming sections on this chapter.

So you are using your keyboard (physical or virtual) to write a statement you intend to disseminate. How does the keyboard, attached to your binary device, accept and pass your human language to the cyber device that does not understand human languages? By acting as the middle-man between the human and the cyber device, by translating the human language input into the binary language understood by the attached cyber device.

In the digital dimension of cyber devices, they understand only two discrete states: on and off, represented by two digits, 0 (off) and 1 (on), thus the term binary system. We refer to each of these states as a bit, the abbreviation for a binary digit, the basic unit of data stored and processed by a cyber device. We group eight bits together to form a byte, and a byte offers the required variety of combinations of 0s and 1s to represent 256 individual characters, including letters of the alphabet, numbers, punctuation marks, and additional characters we use in our human language written communications.

These binary combinations are standardized in coding schemata used to represent data in binary form. There are several iterations of these coding schemata, but perhaps the best known among them is the ASCII schema.[1] These coding schemata allow a human writer to type on a keyboard a statement in human language, and the coding schema will translate it into the corresponding byte sequence that the cyber device is able to store and process.

The ASCII (American Standard Code for Information Interchange) is one of the best known character-encoding schema originally designed to represent the English language, by encoding numerals from 0 to 9, the lowercase set from "a" to "z", the corresponding uppercase set, punctuation symbols, and a set of additional characters required for communication. It encodes 128 specified characters into 7-bit binary integers as shown by the ASCII chart sample below.

Binary	Decimal	Hexadecimal	Glyph
100 0001	65	41	A
100 0010	66	42	B
100 0011	67	43	C
100 0100	68	44	D
100 0101	69	45	E
100 0110	70	46	F
100 0111	71	47	G
....	....	....	....
110 0001	97	61	a
110 0010	98	62	b
110 0011	99	63	c
110 0100	100	64	d
110 0101	101	65	e

1   Others include Unicode and EBCDIC

Binary	Decimal	Hexadecimal	Glyph
110 0110	102	66	f
110 0111	103	67	g

Why did we say that the ASCII coding schema offers encoding for a set of 128 characters? Simply because we are dealing with binary math. Why? Because we are operating in the binary dimension of cyber, and everything is done according to binary math. So, since ASCII normally uses 8 bits (1 byte) to store each character, but the 8th bit is used as a check digit, we actually have only 7 bits available to represent and store each character. In the binary math dimension everything works on the base of 2. Consequently, ASCII provides us with the ability to store a total of 2 to the power of 7, thus resulting in a 128 different values.

How does the I/O device, attached to your binary system, accept and pass your human language to the cyber device that does not understand human languages? By acting as the middle-man between the human and the cyber device, by translating the human language input into binary language.

The ASCII set offers an encoding schema suited primarily for the representation of English characters. It became necessary to adopt extended encoding schemata satisfying the needs for encoding characters beyond the boundaries of the English alphabet, and sets of symbols used outside the United States. Since the advent of the World Wide Web (WWW) the ASCII set, introduced in 1963, remained as the most common character encoding until December 2007. This encoding schema was surpassed by UTF-8, which includes ASCII as a subset, while remaining backward compatible with the 7-bit ASCII set.

The limitations of the ASCII character encoding schema became quite evident with the arrival and growth of the WWW, a global phenomenon for the creation, dissemination and reading of topics of interest to thousands of individuals sharing information on so many different languages. The ASCII character encoding schema could not suffice for the growing population of netizens.[2]

The limitation of the ASCII encoding schema resides in its design limited to represents only English characters. With the expansion of the WWW, other encodings designed to represent other languages created an environments with overlapping codes. So an English language user receiving encoding for a non-English alphabet would obtain a display with corrupted and unintelligent characters. Likewise, a non-English user would experience the same corrupted text when presented with an ASCII encoding set. Thus the search for a unifying encoding set, satisfying all the living language alphabets.

Enter UTF-8. Designed by Ken Thompson and Rob Pike in 1992, UTF-8 is the character encoding schema, capable of satisfying the need for encoding all possible characters used by the many languages on planet Earth. UTF-8 stands for Unicode (or Universal Coded Character Set) Transformation Format, uses 8-bit code units, and it was designed for backward compatibility with the ASCII encoding set.

UTF-8 stands as the dominant character encoding for the WWW, and as of August 2016, it accounts for almost 90% of all Web pages. The World Wide Web Consortium (W3C),[3] the international community responsible for developing open standards to ensure the sustainment and growth of the WWW, recommends UTF-8 as the default encoding in XML and HTML. Likewise, the Internet Mail Consortium (IMC) recommends that all email programs be able to display and create mail using UTF-8. Web developers can use UTF-8 for any language, and even multiple languages at once, and avoid the cumbersome predicament of using language-specific encodings.

Now, let's get back to the keyboard, one of the many devices

---

2   Coined by the merging of the terms "Internet" and "citizen."
3   https://www.w3.org

assisting the input/output (I/O) process in communicating with digital computers. The I/O process consists of various devices and sensors bringing information into the digital computer for processing. The resulting processed data is either stored into digital storage devices or delivered to the output devices assisting the human operating the cyber device, or directly to a secondary system controlled by the computer, as in the case of Industrial Control Systems (ICS) for example. See illustration of I/O model below.

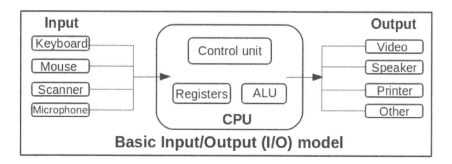

Basic Input/Output (I/O) model

Input devices convert incoming data and instructions into a pattern of binary code for processing. Then the output device reverses the process, translating the digitized signals into a form intelligible to the human user. Input devices include among others keyboards, mice, scanners, and microphones. Output devices include video displays, printers, speakers, and many others.

Let's now consider the amazing convenience of dispensing with the clutter of cables coming out of our keyboard and mouse by transitioning into using wireless keyboards and mice. Isn't that a wonderful thing to do, enjoying the freedom of having a clean and well organized working space without any inconvenient cables getting in the way? However, that convenience comes at the expenses of our cyber security, because we have now added a new risk factor; the potential for the hijacking of the radio signal connecting our new wireless I/O device to our computing device.

Any potential adversary can simply place an online order for a specially designed antenna costing anywhere between $12 to $60, and use it to infiltrate our wireless I/O device. How, you may ask? The cyber attacker can use such antenna to connect to our wireless keyboard, and issue a series of keystrokes commands to activate a browser session, navigate to a particular website, and proceed to download and install malware, or upload data from your hard drive, or simply erase all the data in your hard drive. This is not a hypothetical scenario, but a realistic one.[4]

How, you may ask again? Ah, let's remember the power of interacting with a computing device via CLI, the powerful Command Line Interface. This may come as a surprise to users who know only the GUI interface, so perhaps you may want to explore the exponentially more powerful CLI alternative, to understand how a cyber attacker can infiltrate and control your computing device via CLI.[5]

UTF-8 is the character encoding schema, capable of satisfying the need for encoding all possible characters used by the many languages on planet Earth, and standing as the dominant character encoding for the WWW.

An attacker connecting to a victim's wireless keyboard can compromise even the so-called "air-gapped" computing devices. These are devices with no connectivity to a network, as a condition designed to maintain computing devices safer from cyber attacks delivered through the Internet. However, these devices are unprotected from exploits that can be delivered through a connection to a wireless I/O device, be it a wireless mouse or keyboard.

Some manufacturers responding to the security challenged unveiled by the security researchers attempted – quite predictably – to lower the severity of the attack by claiming

---

4   Ungureanu, Horia. "'Mousejacking' Is A Dangerous Threat That Can Hack Into Your Laptop If You Use A Wireless Mouse." Tech Times.com, 25 February 2016.
http://www.techtimes.com/articles/136206/20160225/mousejacking-is-a-dangerous-threat-that-can-hack-into-your-laptop-if-you-use-a-wireless-mouse.htm

5   Giannelli, Louis. Cyber Reality, 2016, Chapter 8

that the exploit would only work within 10 meters. The researchers proved that the exploit works by injecting keystrokes from 180 meters away.[6]

Some of the affected manufacturers acknowledged the vulnerability, and with the assistance of the security firm unveiling the weakness, have developed and released firmware update for the affected devices. Of course, this updated firmware benefits only users who have applied the said firmware. Have you updated yours?

Oh, wait a second. Are we forgetting something? What about on screen keyboards? Yes, like the one you use every day on your smart phone! You may remember that in 2015 there was a widely publicized Galaxy keyboard security vulnerability, affecting the Galaxy S series, including S4, S5, and S6 phones. The special pre-installed version of the SwiftKey keyboard failed to properly validate language pack updates. The problem with such updates? They were performed by downloading a ZIP archive via an unencrypted HTTP connection, thus providing the opportunity for cyber adversaries to intercept the download and substitute it with a malicious payload.

A successful exploit would allow the attackers the rights to execute malware with system privileges on the affected Galaxy smart phone, and proceed to remotely spying through its camera or microphone. Additionally, the attackers could perform GPS tracking of the victim, install additional malicious apps, and steal information and eavesdrop on the victim's messages and voice calls.

Of course, the security fix for this vulnerability was release in 2015, but in order to receive this security update the affected smart phone needs to be running the KNOX security platform. Have you received and implemented the security update? The best way to have certainty on this issue is to

6   Greenberg, Andy. "Flaws in Wireless Mice and Keyboards Let Hackers Type on Your PC." Wired.com, February 23, 2016, https://www.wired.com/2016/02/flaws-in-wireless-mice-and-keyboards-let-hackers-type-on-your-pc/

contact your carrier. They can show you how to ascertain that your smart phone is securely protected against this exploit.

So, there are ways to maliciously affect the performance of the translator I/O device connected to your cyber device, and by extension to disrupt and/or manipulate the data flow from your I/O device into the processing unit of your cyber devices. Consequently, there are various ways to affect the path of the data flow between the user and the corresponding cyber device. This means we cannot always implicitly trust the data traversing between our I/O devices and the processing unit in our cyber devices.

If you really care about the integrity of the data path between I/O devices and your cyber processing unit, then you need to carefully consider the risks of using wireless I/O devices. Perhaps your cyber security status, and the integrity of your data may be better protected by wired I/O devices? The answer is yours, but so it's the acceptance of the risks associated with the preference of using wireless I/O devices.

And now, just before we move into the next chapter, let's ask ourselves an important question: does the processing and transfer of cyber data actually begins at the keyboard? Does the cyber path originates at this I/O device?

Chapter 2. Threats to the I/O

At the beginning of the previous chapter we call the keyboard the translator, to illustrate the role that this input device plays when a human starts interacting with a cyber system. But does the story of the cyber path really begins at the keyboard? Actually, by the time the user starts typing on the keyboard, this input device is already enable and operational. But how did it become operational?

When the user reach for the power button to apply power to the computer device, how did the keyboard became configured to receive input from the user? How did the keyboard became enabled as a translator?

Enter the BIOS! This is the set of cyber instructions stored in a ROM (read-only-memory) chip. The code instructions stored on a ROM chip are known as firmware, as oppose to the code instructions stored on erasable media, and known as software.

The firmware is responsible for enabling a computer and all its components to become an operational and organized cyber system. The computer without the BIOS would be simply a collection of interconnected electronic devices inside a case, completely useless! How does the computer "becomes aware" of all its separate components? Of course this statement of "becoming aware" in reference to the computer is a literary concession, a euphemistic expression borrowing from an ontological reality the computer does not possess, an ontological reality known only to man.[7]

The Basic Input/Output System (BIOS) is primarily a short series of cyber code instructions designed to facilitate the computer's hardware initialization process. In sequence, this initialization process takes place prior to transitioning control of the cyber system to the operating system (OS). Thus, the

---

7   This author kindly reminds all readers that the generic noun "man" includes both male and female genders.

BIOS essential function is to manage the system setup process immediately after turning the power on.

Modern computers depend on the BIOS cyber instructions. This code is stored in non-volatile memory and is also known as boot firmware. It holds a unique and privilege position within the cyber system's architecture, and, consequently, any unauthorized modification of BIOS firmware by malicious software represents a serious threat. If the BIOS becomes permanently corrupted the entire cyber system becomes disable. The transition from conventional BIOS to implementations based on the Unified Extensible Firmware Interface (UEFI) may render the BIOS into a greater target area, simply because these later BIOS implementations are based on a common set of specifications, thus increasing their target surface.[8]

The process of activating and processing the boot firmware is known as the boot process, which, from a simplified perspective, it includes the following actions: [9]

- it verifies the integrity of other firmware components and trusted computing applications
- it initializes and tests key pieces of hardware on the computer system, including the motherboard, chipset, memory and CPU.
- it initializes other hardware components necessary for booting the system (video card, local area network card, etc).
- it searches for a boot device (hard drive, optical drive, USB drive) and executes the boot loader stored on that device.
- it loads the OS and transfers control of the computer system to the loaded OS.

So, as you can see, the processing and transfer of cyber

8   Cooper, David, et al. "BIOS Protection Guidelines." NIST Special
     Publication 800-147, April 2011.
     http://nvlpubs.nist.gov/nistpubs/Legacy/SP/nistspecialpublication800-
     147.pdf
9   Ibid

data does not begin at the keyboard, but rather in the internal BIOS code. It is this BIOS code that actually enables the computer to "become aware" that it has a keyboard, and capable of receiving and processing the user's input via the keyboard.

Now, since we have identified the BIOS as the beginning of the cyber path, we also have to recognized the BIOS as a critical security item. The BIOS is after all the very first set of cyber code that is executed by the main CPU. We tend to consider that the BIOS should be implicitly trusted, but should it be?

Let's remember that the very moment we apply power to a cyber system the BIOS becomes the general manager and orchestrator of the cyber system. It is responsible for verifying the integrity of firmware and software initialized and executed during the boot process. But it is precisely because of this unique and critical role of the BIOS system that it is regarded as a very attractive attack target. Just imagine the repercussions of the scenario where malicious code is injected at the BIOS level. The malicious code becomes the vector to attack and compromise all components loaded during the booting process. This ominous scenario is not hypothetical, but very real and concrete. An attack on the system's BIOS is an immediate check mate!

Why? Because since the BIOS resides in non-volatile memory, the malicious code written into the BIOS will re-infect the victim system every time is rebooted, even after replacing the infected hard drive, and installing a new OS and AV software. This is because the system BIOS initializes the boot process with very high privileges, leaving very low possibilities for detecting the malicious BIOS code.[10]

The BIOS is very system-specific, and consequently, BIOS exploits are equally specific, targeting a unique version of a system BIOS, directed at potential high-value cyber devices using a particular BIOS version. The transition to UEFI-

---

10   Ibid

based BIOS will simplify and intensify the proliferation of BIOS exploits, since the UEFI-based BIOS implementations are based on common specification. This commonality actually enlarges the target area, rendering more systems vulnerable to exploits targeting a common version of BIOS.

A presentation at Black Hat 2007 was dedicated to introduce the audience into the road map on how to attack the BIOS/EFI variant. The presenter explained that the goal of this type of attack is to subvert the bootloader, which relies on the dynamically created Interrupt Vector Table (IVT). Since the BIOS calls interrupt 19h ("the bootstrap loader" vector), the strategy of this attack is to append the malicious code before this call after IVT is built, and proceed to rewrite IVT to hook the desired interrupt 19h.[11]

The presenter added that the EFI variant offers a large attack surface because of several factors, including vague EFI specification on security, the use of high level development tools (as opposed to assembly language), and the implementation of third party driver model offering an easier target. He concluded by highlighting the fact that UEFI offers plenty of surface for code injection attacks.[12]

Since the BIOS stands at the beginning of the cyber path, we also have to recognized it as a critical security item. The BIOS is after all the very first set of cyber code that is executed by the main CPU. We tend to consider that the BIOS should be implicitly trusted, but should it be?

There have been an abundance of presentations, lectures and demonstrations on BIOS attacks, some of them at venues where this information is disseminated and assimilated by a heterogeneous attendance. While many of

---

11 Heasman, John. "Hacking the Extensible Firmware Interface." Presented at Black Hat USA 2007. https://www.blackhat.com/presentations/bh-usa-07/Heasman/Presentation/bh-usa-07-heasman.pdf

12 Ibid

the presentations are designed to expose exploits, thus improving cyber security, the heterogeneous attendance inevitably includes individuals with diametrically opposite dispositions regarding their plans on how to use the received information.[13]

Historical cases of BIOS-specific attacks, such as the CIH exploit discovered in 1998, targeted the BIOS systems on a specific chipset widely deployed at the time. The designation CIH proceeds from the plain text string inside the malware code, reading: "CIH v1.2 TTIT." This string corresponds to the initials of the malware's author, Chen Ing Hau, from the Taipei's Tatung Institute of Technology.[14]

Eventually, that particular exploit became dated, because it relied on several vulnerabilities no longer present in modern cyber systems. Thus, the transition to common BIOS specifications eliminates the uniqueness of a BIOS system, while at the same time fostering the emergence of more generic new exploits targeting the vulnerabilities inherent in the common BIOS specifications.

While the victim systems could have been recovered to their operational status after replacing the infected BIOS chip, in the late 90s the BIOS chip in most computers were not removable. Therefore, the only practical solution was to replace the entire motherboard. A cursory review of reports on the CIH BIOS exploit will show that numerous reporting organizations mislabeled this exploit as a software affecting files and programs in Windows. This is a gross misrepresentation of the nature of the CIH BIOS exploit. Only a handful of reporting organizations correctly

---

13 Butterworth, John, et al. "BIOS Chronomancy: Fixing the Core Root of Trust for Measurement." Presented at Black Hat USA 2013. https://media.blackhat.com/us-13/US-13-Butterworth-BIOS-Security-Slides.pdf; Kovah, Xeno, et al. "Analyzing UEFI BIOS from Attacker & Defender Viewpoints." Presented at Black Hat USA 2014. https://www.blackhat.com/docs/eu-14/materials/eu-14-Kovah-Analyzing-UEFI-BIOSes-From-Attacker-And-Defender-Viewpoints.pdf
14 Cluley, Graham. "Memories of the Chernobyl virus." NakedSecurity, April 26, 2011. https://nakedsecurity.sophos.com/2011/04/26/memories-of-the-chernobyl-virus/

categorized the CIH threat as a BIOS exploit.[15]

Why is so important to categorize this exploit correctly? Because it attacks the very core of a cyber system, the BIOS system, which, once compromised, creates a scenario where any other additional compromises affecting the OS and files become secondary. There are too many unqualified voices spreading their technically inaccurate opinions on printed media and online fora. These voices lack the proper technical knowledge to capture the essence of cyber exploits, and mislead the public with generalities and erroneous terminologies.

To properly understand the impact of a BIOS exploit is critical in the planning and implementation of the necessary measures to protect critical systems against this type of threat. The CIH exploit will not be the last one targeting the BIOS system.[16] The appeal of launching a cyber attack vector targeting the most critical cyber code residing in the firmware responsible for initializing the target system will never disappear; it is simply a way of inflicting a fatal wound on a target system on a single strike. When a BIOS exploit is successful, the game is over! Does the victim has a contingency plan? Does the victim has the cyber resources required to prepare for this contingency? Regretfully, those who can factually reply in the affirmative are very few.

Cyber systems leak information in unintentional manners, opening a path for a security compromise. Those who are intent in capturing this inadvertent leaks may use the collected information for malicious purposes, such as unlawful or unauthorized intelligence collection. This type of intrusion are known as side-channel attacks, using a variety of information leakages including thermal, electrical and time fluctuations, electromagnetic and acoustic emanations. [17] So,

---

15 Arstecnica.com, InfoSecInstitute.com, and NakedSecurity.sophos.com are among the few who correctly identified CIH as a BIOS exploit.

16 Hruska, Joel. "BIOS-level rootkit attack scary, but hard to pull off." ArsTechnica.com, Mar 24, 2009. http://arstechnica.com/gadgets/2009/03/researchers-demonstrate-bios-level-rootkit-attack/

17 Kelly, Andrew. "Cracking Passwords using Keyboard Acoustics and

let's leave the topic of the BIOS exploits behind for now, and let's focus on another I/O exploit, this ones targeting the previously discussed keyboard device.

An article from Berkeley outlines the new security threat discovered by researchers in 2005, relying on audio recording of the keyboard clicks, leading to uncovering the corresponding data associated with the series of clicks generated by the keyboard data input. Consequently, we are now dealing with an indirect channel of information, requiring no access to the keyboard itself, but to the sound generated by the different keys pressed during the data input.[18]

The Berkeley researchers were able to recover up to 96 percent of the characters selected during the data input sessions, simply by gathering several 10-minute keyboard sound recordings, and performing computer analysis of the recorded audio via an ad hoc algorithm. Though this experiment used a very common and inexpensive microphone located in the room where the typing was taking place, the use of a parabolic microphone allows recording from outside the building, thus increasing the level and effective reach of this type of threat.[19]

The keystroke eavesdropping attack is possible because each key on a computer keyboard produces a slightly different sound when the keyboard support plate is struck in different locations by the different keys. Using a neural network, trained to identify these differences, the eavesdropper can identify which keys had been pressed, based on an audio recording of the typing session under scrutiny.[20]

Language Modeling." University of Edinburgh, School of Informatics, 2010. http://www.inf.ed.ac.uk/publications/thesis/online/IM100855.pdf

18 Yang, Sarah. "Researchers recover typed text using audio recording of keystrokes." UCBerkeley News, 14 September 2005. http://www.berkeley.edu/news/media/releases/2005/09/14_key.shtml
19 Ibid
20 Kelly, Andrew. "Cracking Passwords using Keyboard Acoustics and Language Modeling." University of Edinburgh, School of Informatics, 2010. http://www.inf.ed.ac.uk/publications/thesis/online/IM100855.pdf

An artificial neural network (ANN) is a cyber processing device formed by a number of interconnected nodes, designed to process information according to their dynamic response to external inputs. Essentially, an ANN learns by example, and operates in a different manner than the traditional computer. Computations in a traditional computer proceed according to a series of predetermine instructions stored on a cyber program. Technically, these computational steps are deterministic, sequential and logical.

An ANN, on the other hand, does not execute programed instructions; rather, the multiple processing nodes respond in parallel to the pattern of the external inputs presented to it. ANNs are basically approximators, and they work very well capturing associations, discovering relationships and regularities within a set of patterns.[21]

Cyber systems leak information in unintentional manners, opening a path for a security compromise. Those who are intent in capturing this inadvertent leaks may use the collected information for malicious purposes, such as unlawful or unauthorized intelligence collection.

The emanations of sound waves are not the only means of capturing data from a keyboard. Another side-channel used to capture data from a keyboard is via the emanations of electromagnetic waves generated by a keyboard. This exploit affects both wired and wireless keyboards. A team of researchers demonstrated this exploit in 2009, implementing this type of side-channel attack with a high success rate, recovering 95% of the keystrokes at a distance up to 20 meters. The recovery process succeeded even through walls.[22]

---

21 University of Wisconsin-Madison. "A Basic Introduction To Neural Networks." http://pages.cs.wisc.edu/~bolo/shipyard/neural/local.html
22 Ecole Polytechnique Federale de Lausanne, Compromising Electromagnetic Emanations of Wired and Wireless Keyboards, Vuagnoux, Martin; Pasini, Sylvain. Presented at the 18th USENIX Security Symposium, Montreal, Canada, August 10-14, 2009. http://infoscience.epfl.ch/record/140523?

Whenever the attacker has direct physical access to the targeted keyboard, a more insidious attack can take place, by installing a keylogger on the targeted system. There are both hardware and software keyloggers. In its very essence, keyloggers are legitimate instances of cyber programs designed to capture the keystrokes for troubleshooting or legal monitoring purposes. However, every tool designed for a legitimate purpose is inevitably subverted by malicious actors. Malicious keyloggers have a long history going as far back as 1970.[23]

The traditional side-channels attacks described previously generally apply to physical keyboards, but they are ineffective on soft keyboards such as those employed on touch screen on smartphones and tablet devices. However, these soft keyboards are not necessarily immune to side-channel threats. The motion and vibrations generated on a soft keyboard when touching keys on different locations on the screen become the information required to infer the keys touched by the user. [24]

This new approach to keylogging is based on the variety of sensors for detecting location and motion generated by the touch screen. Those motion sensors, such as accelerometers and gyroscopes, may be used to infer keystrokes, given the close correlation between the keys being typed and the related vibrations on the touch screen. The researchers studying this new side-channel attack were able to infer correctly more than 70% of the keys typed on a smartphone touch screen, using the researchers' original touch screen keylogger application.

Even tough this original app needs to be installed on the victim's smartphone, it is not a difficult task, considering the increasing number of malware apps and untrusted third-

---

ln=en

23   There is a very informative sysnopsis on keyloggers available at: http://en.wikipedia.org/wiki/Keystroke_logging
24   Cai, L., & Chen, H. "TouchLogger: Inferring Keystrokes On Touch Screen From Smartphone Motion." Presented at HotSec 2011, https://www.usenix.org/legacy/event/hotsec11/tech/final_files/Cai.pdf

party code currently available on the smartphone market. Furthermore, the recently published specification to allow web applications access to accelerometer and gyroscope sensors through Javascript (whith Android and iOS support), sets the stage for delivering a motion-based keylogger from a website, without requiring user intervention.[25]

Keyloggers of any kind represent a serious threat to both personal and enterprise cyber security. The cyber path is diverted from its normal course, and redirected to an unauthorized destination, placing data and credentials at risk, and subject to unlawful manipulation and espionage. The unauthorized and unlawful redirection of cyber data can affect any I/O device, and expose private and enterprise information to individuals with malicious intent, threatening personal identities, enterprise cyber security, and national security interests.

Excursus: The GUNMAN Project

For almost a decade, between 1976 to 1984, the former Soviet Union employed electromechanical implants to collect information from the US embassy in Moscow and the US consulate in Leningrad. The information was collected from IBM Selectric typewriters used in those two locations. This espionage case is known as the GUNMAN Project.[26]

The Selectric typewriters used a sphere with alphanumeric characters embossed on the outward spherical surface. The fact that this unauthorized data collection lasted for such long period of time points to two recurrent problems: we tend to underestimate the capabilities of an adversary, and we become complacent and relax in our vigilance. A total of sixteen typewriters were affected by the malicious implants, housed in a modified comb support bar. They used burst

---

25 Ibid
26 Maneki, Sharon A. "Learning from the Enemy:The GUNMAN Project."
    Center for Cryptologic History National Security Agency, 2012.
    https://www.nsa.gov/about/cryptologic-heritage/historical-figures-
    publications/publications/assets/files/gunman-
    project/Learning_From_the_Enemy_The_GUNMAN_Project.pdf

transmission radio frequencies, and an antenna to transmit the data being typed.[27]

The collection procedure used the implants to convert the mechanical energy of key strokes into local magnetic disturbances. The electronic component in the implant responded to these disturbances, categorized the underlying data represented by these disturbances, and transmitted the results to a nearby listening post.

Some of the contributing factors in failing to detect the intrusion included the US use of outdated and inappropriate techniques and equipment during inspections, and analytical mistakes. The burst transmissions were so brief that the signal disappeared from the spectrum before it could be recognized by the outdated spectrum analyzers.[28]

The concealment methodology designed by the Soviets was very ingenious. They used burst transmissions at the 30, 60, or 90 MHZ range radio frequency, the same frequency band as their television stations. This contributed to mask the radio frequency so that US analyzers would miss the transmissions. The NSA Director General Faurer acknowledged in 1986 how people too often tend to become disdainful of their adversaries.[29]

The closing statement on the preceding excursus certainly echoes the famous dictum of the extensively and often misquoted late nineteenth century Spaniard philosopher: "Those who cannot remember the past are condemned to repeat it."[30] Complacency, along with disdain and underestimation of the adversary, are recurrent themes in history.

Keyloggers divert the cyber path from its normal

---

27 Ibid
28 Ibid
29 Ibid
30 Santayana, George. The Life of Reason, Vol. I, Chapter XII. The Project Gutenberg eBook, February 14, 2005. https://www.wikipremed.com/reading/philosophy/The_Life_of_Reason.pdf

course, and redirect it to unauthorized destinations, placing data and credentials at risk, and subject to unlawful manipulation and espionage.

Attacks against the I/O system cover several other categories not discussed in this brief chapter. Its scope is intended to provide a succinct presentation of the many ways in which the cyber path can be subverted and diverted, and more ominously, sometimes without the user's cognizance. There are paths intended for the cyber data to follow when the cyber device is used as intended by the original design. However, we humans always manage to find ways to corrupt the original design in accordance to the inevitable dark side of our human nature.

Is there a perfect technical countermeasure against I/O attacks? No, but there is a mindset that should be cultivated by anyone associated with cyber devices. Vigilance! Constant, relentless, uncompromising vigilance! The cyber dimension is not an entertainment park; it is a fiercely contested environment.

Chapter 3. From Abacus to Von Neumann Model

Human beings have been dealing with computational devices for thousands of year, but only recently, since the 20th century, with electronic computational devices. And yet, regardless of the type of computational device, we have always needed a set of prescribed instructions to implement into the computational device in order to obtain the desired result. A computational device is essentially a calculator, and the early type recorded in history is the abacus, invented in Sumeria circa 2500 BC. Some 2000 years later the Greeks invented another device, the Antikythera mechanism, appearing around 100 BC, both of them well equipped to perform calculations.

Let's now fast forward to the 1900 century, to the time when Charles Babbage invented his Analytical Engine and utilized punched cards to control it. But the birth of the first set of logical and structured instructions, or the first algorithm, was conceptualized and written by the mathematician Ada Lovelace for the Analytical Engine. This accomplishment and methodology led to the advent of the modern development of coding, or computer programming. Ada Lovelace's algorithm earned her recognition as history's first computer programmer.

Excursus: Ada Lovelace

Ada Lovelace holds a place of honor in computing history, since she is regarded as the first computer programmer. As a gifted mathematician, she conceptualized and wrote the instructions for the first computer program in the mid-1800s.

She was born in London on December 10, 1815, the daughter of famed poet Lord Byron, and at an early age she demonstrated an affinity for mathematics, which led to an unusual upbringing for an aristocratic girl in the mid-1800s. Her mother had mathematical training, and arranged for tutors to teach Ada mathematics and science. At the age of 17, Ada met Charles Babbage, a mathematician and inventor, who served as a mentor to Ada. She joined the study of advanced mathematics at the University of London.

At a later date Ada was asked to translate an article written by Italian engineer Luigi Federico Menabrea on Babbage's analytical engine. Ada translated the article to English, and added her own thoughts and ideas on the analytical engine. Her notes became three times longer than the original article, and her work was published in 1843, in an English science journal. Her notes included the first published description of a sequence of operations for solving certain mathematical problems. The concept of a system capable of manipulating symbols in accordance with rules, and numbers representing entities other than quantity led to the fundamental transition from calculation to computation.

Ada's contributions to the field of computer science were not discovered until the 1950s, when they were reintroduced to the world by B.V. Bowden, who republished them in Faster Than Thought: A Symposium on Digital Computing Machines in 1953. Since then, Ada has received many posthumous honors for her work, and in 1980, the US Department of Defense named a newly developed computer language "Ada," in her honor.[31]

Once we conceptualize a particular algorithm, capturing the sequential and logical steps to achieve the desired programmatic goal, we have to express the algorithm in the only language understood by an electronic computer; the binary system. The digital logic and memory devices on an electronic cyber device are based on two electrical states; on and off, thus the binary system, formed with only two symbols, namely 0 and 1.

Each binary digit value constitutes a bit, and a grouping of eight bits is known as a byte. The arithmetic unit in a

---

31 Biography.com. "Ada Lovelace." http://www.biography.com/people/ada-lovelace-20825323; Computer History.org. "Ada Lovelace." http://www.computerhistory.org/babbage/adalovelace/

computer processor is designed to handle a fixed number of bits, known as a "word" in the cyber lexicon. Current computers are designed to handle word lengths of 32 or 64 bits.

Perhaps this is the place to take a brief pause and discuss a few essential details about 32-bit and 64-bit architectures. The number of bits in a processor refers to the size of the data that it can handle, and the size of its registry. A 64-bit processor is capable of accessing over four billion times as much physical memory than a 32-bit processor.

32-bit processors are capable of handling a limited amount of RAM, while 64-bit processors are designed to utilize a much greater amount. However, in order to have access to the greater amount of RAM, the corresponding OS on a cyber system with a 64-bit processor also needs to be designed to handle the available larger RAM.[32]

Regretfully, the majority of authors writing about online information on 64-bit systems tend to think that the whole world runs on the OS marketed by the corporation with headquarters in Redmond, WA., and all their explanations stream from this misconception. While this particular OS may be preferred by users operating simple desktops or laptops for residential and enterprise environments, while running basic-level applications, there is a large percentage of worldwide systems dedicated to more demanding and complex environments, and they operate on Linux. The world does not run on the OS from Redmond only!

While general application computer users may find a 32-bit processor sufficient for general computing tasks, applications requiring larger amounts of memory may need a 64-bit processor to improve performance. Some of these more demanding applications include image and video editing software, and 3D rendering utilities, among others. The expected improved performance, of course, requires the presence of a corresponding 64-bit OS as well, along with 8

---

32   Random Access Memory is a type of volatile data storage in a cyber device.

or 16 GB of RAM.[33]

There are three primary gains on a 64-bit processor: the width of the integer registers and pointers extended to 64 bits, an extended address space available, plus an increased amount of RAM. Why is it that an increase in the number of registers improve computing performance?

In very simple terms, this is the answer. Memory is extremely slow compared to the CPU processing speed, and reading from and writing to memory requires a long time compared to the CPU processing speed. Layers of caches attempt to mitigate this problem, but even the fastest layer of cache is slow compared to internal CPU registers. With more registers present in a 64-bit architecture, more data can be processed internally by the CPU, thus reducing memory accesses and increasing performance.[34]

64-bit environments are also available for Android, since the Android kernel is based on a Linux kernel, and Linux has been supporting 64-bit technology since 2003. My Android Galaxy runs on a 64-bit kernel, and it's possible that many readers' smartphones do so as well. If your Android is running the Lollipop OS version or higher, then your mobile system is running in a 64-bit environment.

The first set of logical and structured instructions, or the first algorithm, was conceptualized and written by the mathematician Ada Lovelace for the Analytical Engine. This accomplishment and methodology led to the advent of the modern development of computer programming. Ada Lovelace's algorithm earned her recognition as history's first computer programmer.

---

33 Bourque, Brad. "The differences between 32-bit vs. 64-bit operating systems explained." Digital Trends, February 9, 2014.
    http://www.digitaltrends.com/computing/32-bit-64-bit-operating-systems/
34 Gayathri M. "64-Bit Android* OS." Intel.com, March 14, 2014.
    https://software.intel.com/en-us/android/articles/64-bit-android-os

Let us now resume our primary discussion on the binary computational system. The conceptualizing of this system is not a modern creation, since there is documented evidence of ancient cultures incorporating binary system in their culture. However, the implementation of the binary system into an electronic device is a modern application of the binary system.

The great 17th century philosopher and father of Calculus, Gottfried Leibniz, derived a system of logic for verbal statements that would be completely represented in a mathematical code, by combining rows of combinations of zeros and ones. Gottfried Wilhelm Leibniz is a German philosopher, mathematician, and logician born in Leipzig.[35] In his 1703 publication "Explication de L'Arithmetique Binaire" Leibniz states that "...reckoning by twos, that is, by 0 and 1, as compensation for its length, is the most fundamental way of reckoning for science, and offers up new discoveries...as numbers are reduced to the simplest principles, like 0 and 1, a wonderful order is apparent throughout."[36]

With the participation of George Boole, the Boolean logic was developed, using the on/off system of zeros and ones for basic algebraic operations. Electronic computers can perform numerous calculating tasks by applying this binary system of logic.[37]

Early 20th century implementations of electronic computers required the use of painstakingly crafted programs, using instructions designed for a particular computer, in binary notation, where every particular computer model would use a set of different instructions, written in machine language

35 This renowned city, that this author has visited on several occasions, counts many other illustrious citizens such as Mendelssohn, Schumann. and Bach

36 Leibnitz, Godefroy-Guillaume. "Explication de l'arithmetique binaire." HAL Id:ads-00104781, 9 Oct 2006. https://hal.archives-ouvertes.fr/ads-00104781/document; Leibniz Translations.com. "EXPLANATION OF BINARY ARITHMETIC." http://www.leibniz-translations.com/binary.htm

37 Binary Translator.com. "What is binary code, the history behind it and popular uses." 2015. http://binarytranslator.com/what-is-binary

(binary system). Each computing system was specifically designed and configured for a single predetermined task, and any change in programming required manual rewiring of the circuits, practically rebuilding the entire system and configuring it for a different task. This resulted in a very tedious and error-prone process, and when mistakes were made, they were difficult to detect and correct.

Thanks to the combined efforts of multiple researches and mathematicians, working either in collaboration or independently, a new model began to emerge, finalizing in the published work of the mathematician and physicist John Von Neumann. Now known as the Von Neumann model, this computer architecture is described in the 1945 First Draft of a Report on the EDVAC. It describes a design architecture for an electronic digital computer consisting of a central processing unit (CPU) containing an arithmetic logic unit and processor registers, and interacting with a control unit containing an instruction register and program counter. This CPU works in conjunction with a memory unit to store both data and instructions, with external mass storage, and with input and output (I/O) devices. The communication exchanged between the CPU, the memory and the I/O takes place through the address, the control, and the data buses. A collection of signal lines connecting all the components in this model is known as a bus. See illustration below for the von Neumann model.

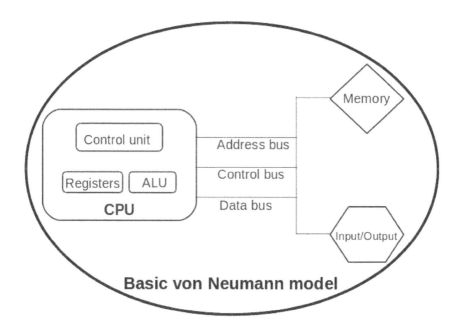

Basic von Neumann model

The CPU is the central element consisting of three main components: the control unit (CU), the arithmetic logic unit, or units (ALUs), and a group of registers. The CU manages the order in which the received instructions should be executed, thus governing the flow of information through the system by issuing control signals to different components. All mathematical and Boolean operations are performed by the ALUs.

The registers perform as temporary storage locations for the transfer of data and instructions in process. The registers, often directly connected to the CU, provide a faster access time than the equivalent access time offered by the memory. Thus, using registers both as the source of operands and as the destination of data results provide a significant performance improvement.[38]

The implementation of the Von Neumann model allowed electronic computers to reach a higher productivity level by enabling computer programs to be stored in computer memory. This versatility avoided the bottleneck represented by the shortcomings of the early fixed-program systems, and launched the era of modern computing. This is the reason

---

38 http://www2.cs.siu.edu/~cs401/Textbook/ch2.pdf

why John Von Neumann is credited as the Father of the Modern Computer. He doesn't stand alone in the path to this accomplishment, but this Hungarian-born American mathematician is credited as the individual who brought to fruition the concept of the basic principle of computer design present in our modern desktops and laptops.[39]

While in Germany, Von Neumann turned his attention to quantum theory, and during the two-year period 1927-29 he practically developed, single-handedly, the entire mathematical foundation of quantum. This pioneering work earned him an invitation to Princeton in 1930, where, along with Albert Einstein, he became one of the six founding mathematics professors of the nascent Institute for Advanced Study.[40]

The impending threat of war ushered in the late 1930s drove Von Neumann to focus on applied mathematics, foreseeing the important role of mathematics in the inevitable conflict. His research in nonlinear partial differential equations, hydrodynamics and the theory of shock waves led to his participation in the Manhattan Project, to develop the first atomic bomb. His research on numerical techniques to solve complex equations led to the need for designing and building computing devices capable of performing the extensive required numerical calculations.[41]

The implementation of the Von Neumann model allowed electronic computers to reach a higher productivity level by enabling computer programs to be stored in computer memory. This model led to the launching of the era of modern computing. This is the reason why John Von Neumann is credited as the Father of the Modern Computer.

---

39 Mathematical Association of America,
     https://www.maa.org/external_archive/devlin/devlin_12_03.html
40 Ibid
41 Ibid

His wartime work during the early Cold War period made Von Neumann in great demand as a consultant to the armed forces. During the 1940s and 50s he was a member of the Scientific Advisory Committee, at the Ballistic Research Laboratories at the Aberdeen Proving Ground in Maryland, a member of the Navy Bureau of Ordnance, a consultant to the Los Alamos Scientific Laboratory, a member of the Armed Forces Special Weapons Project, and a member of the Atomic Energy Commission. The mathematical community elected him as President of the American Mathematical Society from 1951 to 1953. He was awarded the US Medal for Merit in 1947 and the US Medal for Freedom in 1956.[42]

The significance of the introduction of the Von Neumann model resides in the fact that the set of instructions and data are both stored in the same medium. In the original papers proposing this new architecture Von Neumann built his model consisting of five primary components: an arithmetic-logic unit (ALU), a control unit, a memory, some form of input/output, and a bus providing a data communication path between these components. This new architecture eliminates the need for rewiring and rebuilding the computing system when presented with a new task.

The Von Neumann model operates according to the following sequence of operations:

1. In orderly sequence, get the next instruction from memory at the address in the program counter.

2. Add the length of the obtained instruction to the program counter.

3. Proceed to decode the obtained instruction using the control unit, which commands the rest of the computer to perform some operation. Since the obtained instruction may change the address in the program counter, this permits repetitive operations. The change in the program counter may occur only if some arithmetic condition is true, thus

---

42   Ibid

giving the effect of a decision, which can be calculated to any degree of complexity by the ALU.

4. Repeat step 1 until all the instructions in the set have been processed.

The Von Neumann model is simply that: a model. Very few computers operates according to this pristine concept. Instead, modern computers operate on rather modified instances of this model, in order to enhance performance. For instance, the Von Neumann model processes instructions in a single linear sequence, and spends a considerable amount of time moving data to and from the memory. This causes a performance degradation known as the Von Neumann bottleneck. One solution is to modify the model to perform parallel processing, while another enhancement consists on building multiple buses to move instructions and data. However, all such modifications represent simply variations of the original architecture. For all practical purposes, the computer on your desk is a Von Neumann system.[43]

---

43 Ibid

Chapter 4. From Concept to Binary

The path for communication between a human being and a cyber device has already been visited in the previous chapters, specifying the translation process that human language requires in order to become understood by the binary language employed by electronic computers.

Now we need to explore the transformation that occurs through the process of translating a human concept into the set of organized instructions required by an electronic computer. Such process is what we humans need to provide to the cyber devices, in order to enable them for the execution of the particular operations involved in the computer programming sequence designed to accomplish a particular task. We already know that the keyboard becomes the translator, in terms of being the input device linking the human concept into the digital memory and cyber processor, responsible for executing the corresponding instructions. So, where do we start the required transformation process?

The first task is an intellectual project for the individual conceiving a concept designed to create a solution to a particular problem. This first task doesn't involve any cyber device; it involves exclusively the human intellect of conceptualizing and detailing a series of specific, concrete, concise, and sequential logical instructions. There are several degrees of separation between a human concept and the machine language required for a cyber processor to execute a particular task, via the implementation of a series of systematic instructions required to achieve the envisioned and desired results.

Let's now return to the task of understanding the path leading from the computational concept, a purely human conceptualization designed to resolve a problem, to the binary code that the human programmer has to deliver to the CPU. Early computer models would likely use different binary instructions (machine language) to perform a task, but writing such sets of instructions in machine language is obviously a taxing and challenging process. Later, assembly languages were developed that let the programmer specify each instruction in a text format, entering abbreviations for each operation code instead of a binary number, and specifying addresses in symbolic form. The advantage of using program instructions in assembly language is not only more convenient and faster, but also is a process less prone to human error in comparison to the difficult task of writing in machine language.

Assembly language is regarded as the oldest programming language, and as the closest expression to binary machine language as well. Assembly language is used whenever there is a need to obtain direct access to computer hardware. As such, it requires profound knowledge of the specific computer architecture and operating system environment. Consequently, assembly language is designed for a specific processor family, and therefore, not portable to a different processor family.[44]

So, what does it happen after a programmer designs a set of instructions destined to become a computer program? If there are no specific needs for using assembly language, the programmer has many alternatives by selecting any of the available choices among the category of high level programming languages, from the earlies FORTRAN introduced in 1954, to the most recent ones including C, C++, PHP, Java, JavaScript, Perl, Python, Ruby, SQL, and many others.

The term "high level" language describes the capability to write computer programs at a level of abstraction higher than the one allowed by assembly language instructions. Once the source code is written using one of the available high level programming languages, then the programmer uses a special program designed to convert the source code into machine language. This special program, the compiler,

44 Irvine, Kip. Assembly Language for Intel-based Computers, Pearson Prentice Hall, Fifth Edition, 2007

performs the translation from source code into machine language.

There are several degrees of separation between a human concept and the machine language required for a cyber processor to execute a particular task, via the implementation of a series of systematic instructions required to achieve the envisioned and desired results.

At this point in our exploration on the cyber path we should focus on a very succinct but very fundamental question: How does a human being communicate instructions to a microprocessor? Human beings communicate in logical (well, most of the time...) and sometimes intuitive manners. The microprocessor is simply a mathematical calculator capable of processing instructions provided in binary language. And then again, humans do not communicate in binary language, but microprocessors do not understand human languages; they only follow and process instructions written in binary format. Microprocessors do not think; they simple execute instructions in binary language.

In the early days of electronic computing programmers used to provide computing instructions directly in machine language (binary code), but this was not a very efficient and fluid process. We have to remember that there are two primary classes of components in any particular computing devices; the hardware and the software. The former is tangible and concrete, while the latter is virtual, intangible. And yet, it is the latter that offers the means to communicate with the former.

Then, the software component is also present in two classes; low-level software, and high-level software. The former provides a direct interface with the hardware, while the later provides a level of abstraction, isolating the programmer from the hardware, and yet, still able to interact with the hardware through the abstractions provided by high level software, through the facilitator role provided by the low-level software.

Low-level software includes development tools such as compilers, debuggers, and OS, along with low-level programming languages such as assembly language. These low-level software capabilities were not present during the early years of the modern computing age. Today, this low-level software infrastructure greatly facilitates the communication with the computing hardware through the mediating role of modern OS and modern software development tools. This software infrastructure facilitates the isolation of the programmer from the minutiae of the low-level environment, by simplifying the entire process of software development, and greatly increasing productivity.[45]

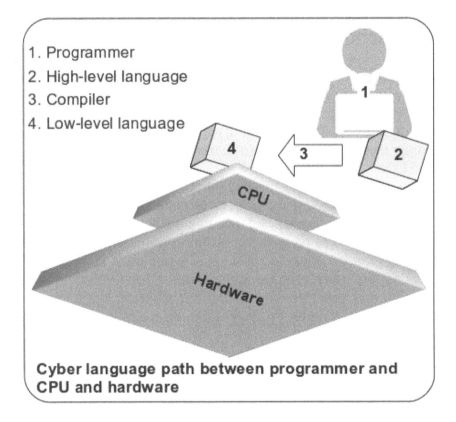

1. Programmer
2. High-level language
3. Compiler
4. Low-level language

Cyber language path between programmer and CPU and hardware

The preceding graphic illustrates the current path in the process of taking a software concept from the mind of a

45 Eilam, Eldad. Reversing: Secrets of Reverse Engineering, Wiley Publishing, 2005

programmer to the electronic computer hardware. The high-level language used by the programmers contains a series of instructions expressed in an abstract manner, tailored to human logic and mentality. The compiler becomes the translator.

When a user interacts with a cyber device is simply interacting with the upper layer of the cyber device, the graphical interface showing text, numbers, graphics, pictures, movies, and playing sounds and music designed to enhance the whole experience of computing. However, below the surface there are many layers of computing components that the average user may never see. At the deepest layer lies the amazingly complex microprocessor, in charge of interacting with all the hardware, coordinating and orchestrating the many sets of instructions handled by the OS.

At the very center of the computing experience is the transistor, that marvelous invention of our electronic age that creates logic gates on an electronic circuit, facilitating the path and the coordination for electrical impulses fluctuating in a predetermined sequence of on and off signals, the very foundation of the binary system. There are only two possible states for any given transistor; on or off, thus, the binary system. The number of transistors have grown exponentially (literally) from a few thousands to billions, thanks to the modern techniques of miniaturization. So, the big question before us is: how does a computer programmer instructs billions of microscopic transistors?

Before we enter into the discussion of this amazing programming phenomenon, let's have a quick review of the progression in both the growing number of transistors in a microprocessor, and the miniaturization process achieved via the modern micro-architecture behind the microprocessor manufacturing. In the next page we are providing a brief synopsis of the different microprocessors produced by Intel in their history, covering the 1971-2012 period.[46]

---

46 Intel Corporation, Transistors to Transformations, 2012

But since the size scale is extremely small, it would be convenient at this point to summarize some measurement standards. In order to do that we have to use the metric system, where the meter is the basic practical standard, based on the decimal system, where every measurement unit is expressed in terms of 10 to the power of (+) x or (-) x.

The metric system is the internationally agreed decimal system of measurement, officially sanctioned for use in the US since 1866. However, the US remains the only industrialized country that has not officially adopted the metric system. Just for the sake of a quick comparison, a meter is slightly longer than a yard, and a millimeter is approximately the thickness of a dime. A meter is expressed as 10^0, a milimeter is 10^{-3}, a micron is 10^{-6}, and a nanometer is 10^{-9} (abbreviated as "nm"). The following table illustrates the progression in terms of the amount of transistors in Intel microprocessors, and the extreme miniaturization of the transistors, in a reversed proportion; the more transistors in a chip corresponds to an extremely microscopic scale, reaching the nanoscale, which is in the 0.000000001 range, or one-billionth of a meter

Year	Intel Chip model	Transistors	Micro-architecture
1971	4004	2,300	10 micron
1972	8008	3,500	10 micron
1974	8080	4,500	6 micron
1978	8086	29,000	3 micron
1982	286	134,000	1.50 micron
1985	386	275,000	1.50 micron
1989	486	1.2 million	1.00 microm
1993	Pentium	3.1 million	0.80 micron
1995	Pentium Pro	5.5 million	0.35 micron
1997	Pentium II	7.5 million	0.25 micron
1999	Pentium III	9.5 million	0.25 micron
2000	Pentium 4	42 million	0.18 micron
2003	Pentium M	55 million	90 nm
2006	Core 2	291 million	65 nm
2008	Core 2	410 million	45 nm
2010	2nd generation	1.16 billion	32 nm
2012	3rd generation	1.4 billion	22 nm

Let us now refocus on the main topic, which is the transition from a human concept into a series of instructions designed to resolve a problem via operations in binary language. The task of finding the solution is passed to a microprocessor, which is simply a mathematical calculator capable of processing instructions provided in binary language. The methodology of processing this transition is based on the creation of an intermediary language, that would facilitate the capturing of a human concept, and translating it into binary instructions for the microprocessor. Enter programming.

Humans do not communicate in binary language, and microprocessors do not understand human languages; they only follow and process instructions written in binary format. Microprocessors do not think, and they do not have intelligence; they simple execute instructions in binary language.

Programming is the arrangement of orderly sets of logical instructions for a microprocessor to follow and process in a particular order. The instructions are provided as binary sequences arranged in the format compatible to the type of microprocessor that will execute the binary sequences. Not all processors are created equally, and perhaps one of the most distinctive difference is the manner in which a processor manages the amount of data made available for calculations.

Binary values are usually arranged into sets of 8 bits, known as a byte. In this section we will cover only general purpose processors, designed primarily for personal use, and different from those designed for industrial use. Some of the early general purposes microprocessors include the Intel 4004, introduced in 1971, and capable of processing only 4 bits at a time. Then the Intel 8080 appeared in 1974, offering the residential market an upgraded microprocessor designed with an 8-bit data width bus. Since then we have seen upgrades to 16-bit, 32-bit, and currently 64-bit data width buses. Of course, a 64-bit data width bus will require the corresponding 64-bit OS to benefit from the improved performance offered by a 64-bit computing environment.[47]

The size of the data width bus is one of the determining factors in the performance of a microprocessor. 32-bit and 64-bit architectures determine the maximum lengths of binary units, or bits that can be computed at one time. Therefore, a 64-bit processor can process twice the amount of bits than a 32-bit processor at any one time. It follows that sets of instructions that are 64-bit in length cannot be processed by a 32-bit processor. The advantage in speed on a 64-bit processor is added to the maximum amount of RAM supported by a 64-bit processor. By comparison, a 32-bit processor supports a maximum of near 4GB of memory, whereas a 64-bit computer can support memory amounts in excess of 4 GB.

The issue of the amount of memory supported by a 64-bit processor is a little bit more complicated, because there are other factors that come into play. In theory a 64-bit processor can address memory space equal to 2^{64}, which translates into 16.8 million terabytes, or 16 exabytes (18,446,744,073,709,551,616 bytes). However, are all the other main components in a computer capable of handling this enormous amount of memory? There are no current chips designed to allow accessing this enormous amount of addressable memory. Furthermore, do we have a motherboard capable of hosting such amount of memory modules? And do we have a current operating system capable of managing this large amount of memory? And again, where would we find the memory modules totaling 16.8 million terabytes? That's why we can say that a 64-bit microprocessor is capable of supporting memory amounts in excess of 4 GB, but the actual count can only be determine in conjunction with the memory support available from the other components mentioned in this paragraph.

---

47 My personal computer, for instance, is a Linux system with a 64-bit high-performance quad-core microprocessor Intel i7, and a 64-bit OS.

So, the bottom line is this. A 64-bit microprocessor is capable of addressing a much larger memory than a 32-bit microprocessor, but the other computing factors in the particular system hosting the 64-bit processor will actually determine how much memory above 4 GB are addressable in that particular system. However, when all the other components in a computing environment become capable of addressing memory above 1 terabyte, then the 64-bit processor will not need to be upgraded, because is already capable of handling a larger addressable memory.

Before we continue, we need to have a word about a WORD. Of course, this is a pun intended! This is necessary because we are trying to find our way on how to translate a human concept into a binary program. Part of the task is to create a bridge between two completely different languages; human language, and digital language.

When it comes to digital processors, we have to define the architecture of this digital workhorses. In human language a word is a unit of thought, an expressed concept designed to convey, by itself or in combinations with additional words, a particular conceptual meaning. On the other hand, a WORD in computing architecture represents a unit of data, with a defined bit length, that can be addressed, and also moved between the computer storage and the computer processor. Remember that we recently mentioned the data width bus? Customarily, the defined bit length of a word (a unit of data) is equivalent to the width of the computer's data bus. Under this condition, and in a single operation, a word can be moved from the computer storage to a processor register.

A word, therefore, can contain multiple computing items, including a computer instruction, or a storage address, or application data subject to manipulation. Some processor designs also support double word instructions, address, or application data. In general terms, there is a direct relationship between the word length and the performance capacity of a processor in a single operation. Thus, the word length is a very important factor in any specific processor designed for computer architecture. Most modern general purpose computers usually operate on either 32 or 64-bit environments. As a general statement, the longer the word length on the architecture of a microprocessor, the more computational work that processor can accomplished in a single operation.

Programming directly in binary language, or machine language (ML) is very difficult, leading to a large percentage of programming errors, which are also very difficult to detect. The closer we can get to the native computer binary language is via assembly language (AL). In AL programming the sets of instructions are briefly stated in a basic abstraction pattern represented by mnemonics, or alphanumerics symbols. However, AL programs must be translated to ML before they can be stored and executed by the microprocessor. We use an assembler to translate the mnemonics into the bit patterns, and this assembler output is placed in memory for the microprocessor to execute the program. The assembler is a cyber program that automates the conversion of mnemonics into ML, that is, into binary language.

Programming is the arrangement of orderly sets of logical instructions for a microprocessor to follow and process in a particular order. The instructions are provided as binary sequences arranged in the format compatible to the type of microprocessor that will execute this binary sequences.

AL mnemonics consist of abbreviated instructions provided to the processor, in order to carry the program instructions. The essence of the calculations can be simplistically summarized as a series of operations involving values transferred between register and memory addresses. For instance, if we have a series of registers labeled R5 through R9, and memory addresses labeled x9000 through x9008 (in hexadecimal notation), then we can have a short series of instructions, expressed in the format "instruction destination, source; comment," such as the following example:

mov.w R5, R6   ;move the content on R6 to R5

The rest of the program will consist of a long series of similar instructions for data transfers and calculations. There are several other mnemonics such as ADD, PUSH, JMP (jump), CMP (compare), etc.

So, from a simplified model point of view, the transition from a human concept into ML code supplied to the microprocessor may follow the following steps:

1. The programmer creates an algorithm containing the methodical and concise series of instructions required to achieve the desire computing solution.
2. The algorithm is translated into a high level programming language (C, C++, PHP, Java, JavaScript, Perl, Python, etc)
3. A compiler will take the high level instructions and translate them into ML

There is, however, an alternate course of action. If a required computing solution needs the set of instructions expressed in AL format, then an assembler will translate AL instructions into ML instructions. For example, the AL instruction ADD R5, R4 is translated into 0100 0110 0000 0101

There are specific circumstances when both the knowledge and availability of AL are still very much needed. These circumstances include environments when hand-craft code with exceptional speed is required, in combination with a low demand for memory. There are also environments where the programmer requires total control of the code performance, such as in the case of low-level drivers or embedded applications requiring the highest levels of performance. Finally, when the time comes for performing reverse-engineering operations, and no access to the source code is available, AL knowledge and expertise prove to be invaluable.

Let's attempt to summarize the purpose of this chapter by using simplified diagrams of the flow of the transition process from a human concept into binary language, to be processed by a microprocessor, in order to obtain a computing solution.

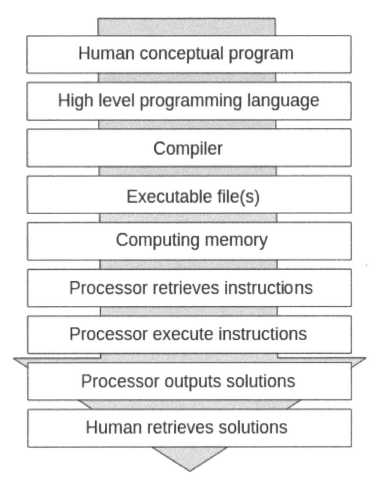

Generic Transition Model Diagram

This is only a simplified generic representation of the flow of the main aspects of the transitional flow. The diagram is an abstraction of the entire process, and does not attempt to provide technical details.

During the process of transforming a human concept into binary language there are two main avenues. One that follows a more expeditious path by using a high level programming language, and depending on a compiler to translate the high level language into binary language.

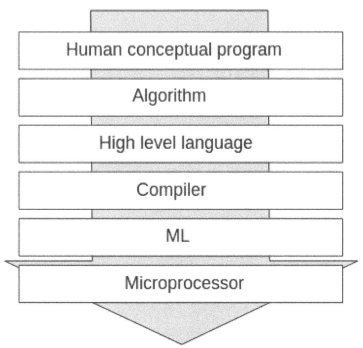

Transition Model Diagram with High Level Language

This model is the most commonly used, since it offers the advantages of expediting the process of translation, and therefore offer also cost saving effects in the production of the binary code. And if the high level language is properly translated by the compiler there will be no problems. However, if something goes wrong with the compiler, and there is an urgent need for locating and correcting the programming flaw, then is when we look at the alternative …

Yes, the use of AL is undoubtedly more costly and time consuming, but the amount of control the programmer can exercise over the set of instructions is unparalleled. For this reason, having a set of instructions in AL will render a high level of control in revising, detecting errors, and correcting them in less time and with cost saving effects. Besides, as we already stated it, there are environments where AL coding is a requirement.

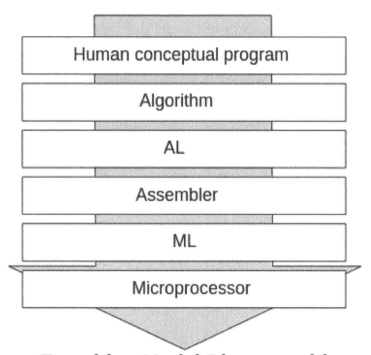

Transition Model Diagram with Assembly Language

There may be many high level language programmers who may consider AL either obsolete or undesirable. However, a programmer who knows both high level language programming and AL programming, will be always a step ahead of the one who knows only the former but not the latter.

This transitional process of translating a human concept into a set of binary instructions, that can be processed by a cyber system operating at the binary language level, is perhaps one of the most effective and elegant solutions envisioned, designed and implement by a few brilliant individuals, for the benefit of the many. This process has virtually and concretely changed our global existence in so many positive ways. At the same time, this very same process has contributed to the unleashing of the dark side of humanity, always present, always lurking, to trample on the good intentions of the few creators, and transform this cyber environment into a field of iniquity and destruction.

Chapter 5. The Microprocessor Path

The intellect, ingenuity and creativity of men and women in the United States of America constitutes the cradle of every seminal, major core accomplishment in the essential building blocks of the cyber dimension. And none is more seminal and essential than the microprocessor, the cyber device at the very center of the core of the cyber dimension. America is the nation bestowing the gift of the cyber spectrum to the rest of the world. Other nations and individuals have contributed with enhancements in the cyber dimension, but the core elements of the cyber dimension first saw the light in the US.

Who invented the microprocessor? There were several people who conceived the idea almost simultaneously, but the one receiving the recognition for its creation is the engineer Ted Hoff (along with the co-inventors Mazor and Faggin) working for Intel Corp., in California.

During the decades 1950s and 1960s the microprocessor CPUs were built with multiple chips. During the late 60s many had written about the conceptualization of a computer on a single chip, but the consensus then considered that integrated circuit technology was not feasible at that time. Ted Hoff was probably the first to focus on Intel's new silicon-gated MOS (Metal Oxide Semiconductor) technology and postulate that, along with a sufficiently simple architecture, it might facilitate the development of a single-chip CPU. [48]

During the late 60s and early 70s there were several American companies competing for the design, manufacturing and marketing of a single-chip microprocessor. In 1969 Intel, then a start-up company dedicated to the manufacturing of memory chips, received a contract from the Japanese company Busicom to work on the next generation of programmable calculators. Intel assigned engineers Ted Hoff, Federico Faggin and Stan

---

48 http://history-computer.com/ModernComputer/Basis/microprocessor.html

Mazor to work with the Japanese Busicom engineer Masatoshi Shima in this project. Busicom initially proposed the production of a 7-chip set, but Hoff argued that this design was not cost effective, since it was too complex. Hoff countered with a design based on a 4-chip set, and Intel was now committed to the first single-chip CPU, the 4004.

Federico Faggin headed the design team, and nine months later, (really, it's not a joke) a revolutionary chip was born, consisting of 2,300 P-MOS (Metal Oxide Semiconductor) transistors, in an area of about 3 by 4 millimeters, using 10micron manufacturing technology. The novel Intel 4004 chip had as much computing power as the ENIAC,[49] which covered 3000 cubic feet with 18000 vacuum tubes. The Intel 4004 used binary-coded decimal arithmetic on 4-bit word, executed about 100,000 instructions per second, had a 45 command instruction set, a register set containing 16 registers of 4 bits each, and performed basic addition and subtraction.

The concept of a computer-on-a-chip is a combination of a microprocessor core (CPU), some memory, and I/O, all on one chip. Intel manufactured the first 8-bit microprocessor and marketed it as the 8080 in 1972. in January 1975 the Altair 8800 went on the market, becoming the first successful personal computer, featuring the new and powerful 8080 microprocessor, thus becoming the industry standard, capable of executing 290,000 instructions per second, and offering 64K bytes of addressable memory. Intel was not alone in the microprocessor market, and there were several other contemporary versions of microprocessors, and by 1976 there were other manufacturers offering 16-bit microprocessors, along with Intel. The world's first single-chip fully-32-bit microprocessor when on production in 1982.[50]

Since the first 8-bit 4004 microprocessor in 1971, Intel has

---

49 Built between 1943 and 1945, the ENIAC (Electronic Numerical Integrator And Computer) was the first large-scale electronic computer. http://www.computerhistory.org/revolution/birth-of-the-computer/4/78

50 http://history-computer.com/ModernComputer/Basis/microprocessor.html

maintained an uninterrupted series of upgrades and improvements to the microprocessor family, ranging from 32-bit and 64-bit microprocessors. From the early chips labeled as part numbers (8086, 80386, or 80486), along with the common designator "x86 architecture," newer designators comprised names such as Pentium, Celeron, CoreTM, and Intel AtomTM processors. Data paths have also evolved, from 8 bits to 32 bits, 64 bits, and 128 bits and beyond, while operating frequencies grew from a few megahertz to 2 GHz (two billion cycles per second) and beyond.[51]

Intel microprocessor architecture offers the Intel CoreTM i7 processor (high-performance) and the Intel AtomTM processor (low-power) implementations. It also offers chips with multi-core performance, where two or more processor cores operate within a single chip, and multi-threading, allowing a single core to perform multiple tasks to improve performance. Normally, the processor works in conjunction with compatible support chips. In general terms, an Intel architecture include two major components: the microprocessor chip, and the support chip PCH (Platform Controller Hub).

In earlier architectures Intel processors operated with two companion chips, known as the "north bridge" and the "south bridge." Currently, the functions of the former are assimilated in the processor itself, while the latter is replaced by the more capable PCH; this is known as the two-chip set configuration. There is a single-chip (SoC) configuration, where the functions of the PCH are included in the processor itself. The former is designed for higher performance and expansion capability, while the latter is optimized for small size and low cost. Do you know what type of microprocessor architecture is in your PC? The name of the processor in your PC will give you the answer.

The Intel Core i7 processor is a quad-core high-performance system, a high-end 64-bit implementation. Each one of the four CPUs has its own L1 and L2 caches, and access to the shared L3 cache. The processor's on-chip DRAM controller

51   Intel, White paper Introduction to Intel Architecture, Jim Turley, 2014

maintains cache coherence. If data at a particular requested address is not present in one of the processor's caches, or if the data in external memory is newer than the cached copy, then the memory controller receives the instruction to retrieve the data at the requested address. Data transfers between the processor and memory are always on a 64-bits wide path. Intel's Direct Media Interface (DMI) is the high-speed bus linking the Intel Core i7 processor and its companion chip, the PCH. See diagram below.[52]

Processor Graphics	Core	Core	Core	Core	System Agent, Display Engine, Memory Controller
	Shared L3 Cache				
	Memory Controller I/O				

Simplified illustration of Intel CoreTM i7 processor internal configuration

The Intel architecture system requires a boot ROM, the BIOS, to bootstrap the processor, load an OS and configure components. Many Intel architecture platforms come with the necessary boot firmware already installed, but in the case of custom or updated systems, Intel offers its Intel Boot Loader Development Kit, which can be used to create a UEFI-compliant boot loader compatible with several operating systems. Where a more minimally functional boot loader may suffice, the Intel Firmware Support Package FSP is available.

The Intel Atom processor is a recent addition to the Intel architecture family of 32-bit processors, designed for deployment on embedded systems where small size, modest power consumption, and low cost are important requirements. The Atom processor offers small size with high

52 Ibid

The intellect, ingenuity and creativity of men and women in the United States of America constitutes the cradle of every seminal, major core accomplishment in the essential building blocks of the cyber dimension.

Let us now transition into the issue of cyber threats at the microprocessor level, since in a previous chapter we already briefly examined some of the BIOS threats. Should we consider that once the cyber code and cyber data arrives at the microprocessor all the threats encountered at the BIOS level are no longer an issue? Such consideration would be in error, because new forms of threats are also present at the microprocessor level. Is there any step in the cyber path were threats are not present? Absolutely not. The threats against the cyber code and the cyber data are present along the entire journey, from origin to destination.

A cyber device has the ultimate purpose of executing the set of instructions residing on a loaded cyber program, and to process the corresponding data provided in that same cyber program, jointly entrusted to the microprocessor. On some occasions the provided cyber data appears in a fixed, static format, while on others in a dynamic format, dependent on user's input. Sometimes it appears in a hybrid format, mixing both static and dynamic data. The program scheduled for execution by the processor requires to store the corresponding data on a specific memory location, and it is this very requirement that becomes the catalyst for the emergence of new cyber threats.

The memory on any cyber device is finite. Therefore, unless the programmer explicitly designs and enforces the boundaries for any segment of memory responsible for executing the program, violations to the memory boundaries will create conditions fostering cyber threats. The size and length of the data allowed to be stored into memory

---

53 Ibid

becomes the critical issue. When the size of data stored in memory is greater than the size allocated for a corresponding memory segment, the result is the dreaded "Buffer Overflow" (BOF) condition.

Though the cyber terminology used to describe a BOF may appears difficult to the uninitiated, a BOF is quite simple, when considering the analogy of a glass of milk; a 4-ounce glass of milk cannot hold 8 ounces of milk. When you pour the 8 ounces into the glass you will have a mess in your hands; the glass will overflow.

When a programmer reserves memory for a program, this reserved memory space is often called a buffer. Thus, when we violate this condition, knowingly or unknowingly, we create a BOF.

The CPU holds a number of registers, which can hold and process the data associated with the program loaded into the CPU. One register in particular is the instruction pointer (IP), responsible for monitoring the progress according to the intended orderly execution of the program. The IP keeps information on the address for the next instruction scheduled for execution. This is the expected normal procedure for the orderly execution of a given program.

However, we may encounter conditions under which this orderly process is altered, in order to execute an spurious instruction, introduced with nefarious intentions. A very notorious presentation published in 1996 is perhaps one of the most well-known cases of introducing a guideline to inject a malicious instruction into the buffer, in order to disrupt the execution of a legitimate program, and take control of the targeted microprocessor.[54]

However, the seminal BOF paper from 1996 is not the first instance of recognizing this programming error. The recognition of this data integrity problem occurred as early

---

54 Bugtraq, r00t, and underground.org, Smashing The Stack For Fun And
    Profit, Aleph One

as 1973, and the first documented exploit in 1988.[55]   The stack referenced in the 1996 paper is a temporary holding place in memory, containing the return address pointer identifying the next instruction to be executed. This arrangement of a pointer is critical to maintain the orderly execution of the program loaded into the memory of the microprocessor; it points to the next executable code instruction waiting on the stack for its turn to achieve execution. If a program is not designed to check buffer boundaries, then a BOF will occur whenever the size of data loaded into the buffer exceeds the size of the buffer itself. If the program failing to check boundaries runs with elevated privileges, then we are compounding the problem, because the attacker successfully exploiting the BOF vulnerability will simply gain elevated or root privileges in the compromised system.[56]

In the most common type of stack overflow the function pointers are overwritten in order to alter the program flow, or gain elevated privileges within the operating system environment. In any standard program we find two basic components; text and data. The former constitutes the actual read-only code in machine-readable format, while the latter encompasses the information for the execution flow of the text component as it follows the execution instructions. When the OS loads the executable, the text component is loaded first into memory, followed by the data component.

Is there a way to protect a cyber system from the dreaded threat of a BOF? Yes, there is. However, the reader must be reminded that any defensive strategy and implementation is inevitably followed by a counter strategy and implementation. Nothing is perfect or impugnable in the cyber dimension; there are only cycles or victory and defeat.

The BOF attack is based on vulnerabilities allowing the introduction of memory corruption, resulting in the execution

---

55 SANS Institute InfoSec Reading Room, Inside the Buffer Overflow Attack:Mechanism, Method, & Prevention, Mark E. Donaldson, April 3, 2002
56 Syracuse University, Buffer-Overflow Vulnerabilities and Attacks, Lecture Notes

of arbitrary code. This attack is implemented by redirecting the program flow to a writable memory area containing instructions defined by an attacker . Therefore, the defensive strategy against the BOF attack consist of a configuration of the memory in such a manner as to render the target memory area more difficult to detect and manipulate. The unpredictability of the target memory is defined in cyber terms as increasing the entropy of the memory configuration.

This increment in the entropy is known as the Address Space Layout Randomization (ASLR). The ASLR is a memory-protection process for operating systems (OSes), designed as a protective strategy to offer another layer of protection against BOF attacks. The principle implemented via ASLR consist of randomizing the location where system executables are loaded into memory.

ASLR was pioneered by the Linux PaX project, which coined the term "ASLR", and published the first design and implementation of ASLR in July 2001. It is seen as the most complete implementation, providing also kernel stack randomization since October 2002. Compared to other implementations, it is also considered as providing the best layout randomization.

Now, let's consider another avenue of threats to the microprocessor. Is there another alternate way to introduce malicious modifications or alterations to the microprocessor? The attack to the memory of the processor presupposes there is already an installed processor on a computing device, and we will use the BOF type of attack to subvert the computing system. However, there is a more insidious way of planning an attack to the microprocessor, and that is during the many manufacturing steps leading to the final product, threatening the integrity of the microprocessor even before it is installed into a cyber system.

The microprocessor constitutes the most vulnerable component in any cyber device. Why? Because the microprocessor resides at the lowest, most fundamental hardware foundation in our classical computing model. Everything else depends on the proper performance of the microprocessor, and it doesn't matter what kind of protection we may plan to protect the other computing layers, if the foundation collapses, that is, the microprocessor, then everything else collapses as well. Perhaps the most dangerous misconception regarding cyber security is to consider the microprocessor as the foundation of trusted computing. This faulty assumption has the same roots as trusting Internet protocols. In the beginning of the computing age we design and manufactured all microprocessors and supporting components in the USA, during the age of innocence, when computing was a close dimension between trusted partners. This is no longer the case. The age of innocence in computing no longer exist.[57] We live in the age of contested computing, the age on untrusted computing.

The figure below illustrates the interaction between the four basic layers in a cyber system, with all three upper layers depending on the microprocessor, representing the proverbial Achilles heel.

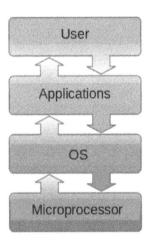

The user depends on the applications (software) to accomplish a variety of computing tasks, and the applications depend on the OS to provide the interactions

57 Giannelli, Louis. The Cyber Equalizer. Chapter3. The Age of Innocence. 2012

between the required computing tasks and the microprocessors capabilities. However, the microprocessor is the end of the line, and thus, everything depends on it. When adversarial actions intrude into the applications and/or the OS, there are corrective actions leading to a recovery path, in terms of eradicating the effects of the adversarial activities on these two layers. However, when adversarial activity affects the microprocessor, there are no recovery alternatives; it is check mate, and the game is over!

Is there a way to protect a cyber system from the dreaded threat of a BOF? Yes, there is. However, the reader must be reminded that any defensive strategy and implementation is inevitably followed by a counter strategy and implementation. Nothing is perfect or impugnable in the cyber dimension; there are only cycles or victory and defeat.

In order to better understand the threats to a microprocessor, it is also vital to understand some of the factors involved in the manufacturing of a microprocessor. Because this is a lengthy, extremely challenging and expensive process, the manufacturing process is never initiated and completed at a single geographical location. Economical factors dictate that the manufacturing process is divided among several global locations, in order to render this process economically viable.

The US government cannot sustain the private manufacturing of microprocessors, so it must depend on commercial manufacturers with the dedicated personnel and specialized facilities. These private companies have to secure a financial model that allows them to stay within acceptable and efficient profitability margins, and in doing so, they have to create partnerships supporting these profitability margins. The bottom line? The manufacturing of microprocessors, by necessity, is a multi-player business, with each one of the players having national interests to protect. So, to say the least, the technical and financial demands for manufacturing microprocessors are also accompanied by the dynamics of national agendas held by the multi-players in the microprocessor manufacturing state of affairs.

First, let us attempt to examine a cursory review of the technical difficulties in the manufacturing challenge of microprocessors, popularly referenced as chips. Obviously, the best data for this exercise comes from the US national manufacturer Intel.

The entire manufacturing process for microprocessors is a very complex series of operations requiring hundreds of precisely controlled procedures, resulting in patterned layers of various materials. The multi-layer arrangement of transistors and interconnects (electrical circuits) on a silicon wafer is achieved through a photolithographic "printing" process. A single wafer holds hundreds of identical processors created through this procedure. Though manufactured microchips may have a flat appearance, they contain three-dimensional structures, including as many as 30 layers of complex circuitry.[58]

The microprocessor constitutes the most vulnerable component in any cyber device. Why? Because the microprocessor resides at the lowest, most fundamental hardware foundation in our classical computing model.

The beginning step in the creation of chips begins with the creation of tiny patterns on a polished 12-inch silicon disk, through a process known as photolithography, where a series of very thin layers of materials are deposited on the surface of the silicon disk, the wafer.[59]

---

58 Intel. "From Sand to Circuits." Retrieved on 22 Nov 2016. http://www.intel.com/content/www/us/en/history/museum-making-silicon.html

59 Chafkin, M, & King, I. "How Intel Makes a Chip." Bloomberg.com, June 9, 2016. http://www.bloomberg.com/news/articles/2016-06-09/how-intel-

Over a period of months these wafers will become microprocessors, through a process of more than 2,000 steps of lithography, etching, material application, and additional etching. The individual chips will then be cut from the wafer into multiple thumbnail-size "dies," and each of them will be encased into a ceramic enclosure.

The size of the chip constitutes another technical difficulty, especially when it comes to the core element, the transistor. A microprocessor is essentially made of transistors, playing the role of a switch, activated by small electrical pulses. The miniaturization of transistors is perhaps one of the greatest challenges in the manufacturing of a chip. Just consider the extreme miniaturization of the transistors in the most current state of the art microprocessor, the Xeon E5, containing 7.2 billion transistors, measuring only 14nm, and introduced in late 2014. By comparison, a human red cell is 7,000nm in diameter, an a biological virus is 100nm.

Let's now briefly consider the expenses associated with chip manufacturing. The development and manufacturing of a new microprocessor is one of the riskiest and expensive business endeavors. Just the building of a manufacturing facility capable of producing a chip like the Xeon E5 demands an investment of at least $8.5 billion. This doesn't include the costs of R&D (over $2 billion) or the cost of the circuit layout design, at over $300 million). The Xeon E5 retails for over $4,000. The reader may be benefiting from the E5 performance whenever conducting searches on Google.[60]

Intel sustains its technical lead in the microprocessor business by maintaining a global manufacturing and assembling network. Accordingly, it is precisely through this unavoidable economical model of global manufacturing that another threat against the microprocessor emerges.

makes-a-chip
60   Ibid

According to data posted on the Intel website,[61] Intel maintains 9 wafer fabrication sites and 7 assembly test manufacturing locations worldwide. Wafer fabrication for microprocessors and chip sets is conducted in US locations (Arizona, New Mexico, Oregon and Massachusetts), and overseas locations in China, Ireland and Israel. After the components are manufactured, they are assembled and tested at facilities located in China, Costa Rica, Malaysia, and Vietnam.

I can't resist the temptation of being sardonic at this time. Do you think that this situation might offer the opportunity for introducing cyber threats into the production of microprocessors and chip sets?!

When adversarial actions intrude into the applications and/or the OS, there are corrective actions leading to a recovery path, in terms of eradicating the effects of the adversarial activities on these two layers. However, when adversarial activity affects the microprocessor, there are no recovery alternatives; it is check mate, and the game is over!

When it comes to microprocessors and their associated electronic components, counterfeiting becomes not only a cyber threat, but a threat to national security as well. This is a fact clearly outlined in previous governments reports, and reiterated in the latest GAO report in 2016.[62]

This reports states that the DoD supply chain is vulnerable to the threat of counterfeit parts. Since 2013-2014, DOD began requiring its agencies and contractors to report on suspect counterfeit products. The reporting vehicle is known as

---

61 Intel. "Intel Global Manufacturing Facts." Retrieved on 22 November 2016. http://download.intel.com/newsroom/kits/22nm/pdfs/Global-Intel-Manufacturing_FactSheet.pdf

62 GAO (United States Government Accountability Office). "COUNTERFEIT PARTS. DOD Needs to Improve Reporting and Oversight to Reduce Supply Chain." GAO-16-236, Report to Congressional Committees, February 2016. http://www.gao.gov/assets/680/675227.pdf

GIDEP, the Government-Industry Data Exchange Program. According to DoD's Counterfeit Prevention Policy, a counterfeit item is defined as "an unauthorized copy or substitute that has been identified, marked, or altered by a source other than the item's legally authorized source and has been misrepresented to be an authorized item of the legally authorized source."[63]

Of course, even though a variety of items are at risk of being counterfeited, our concern in this particular context includes microelectronic components used in national defense systems, such as fighter jets, and guidance systems.

Although the Defense Logistic Agency (DLA)'s primary responsibility is to provide logistical support for thousands of weapon systems enabling the mission of our military services, this GAO 2016 reports states that "it is likely that DLA is not reporting all of the suspect counterfeit parts detected in GIDEP as suspect counterfeit parts. including testing for suspect counterfeit parts." However, DLA is properly equipped to perform the detection of counterfeits, with test centers at two locations capable of conducting electronic testing, along with mechanical, analytical and chemical tests.[64]

The Army, the Air Force and the MDA (Missile Defense Agency) did not submit any suspect counterfeit GIDEP reports because they rely on their contractors to submit such reports, considering they have the best information regarding the origin of the procured counterfeit parts. For the period 2011-2015, GAO found that of the 526 reports of suspect counterfeit parts entered in GIDEP, over 90 percent of these reports were submitted by contractors.

Many years before the publication of the 2016 GAO report we received the studious and frequently cited paper advising the cyber technical community about the threat imposed on the supply chain by the globalization model.[65]

---

63 Ibid
64 Ibid
65 Adee, Sally. "The Hunt for the Kill Switch." IEEE Spectrum, May 2008.

Given the enormous amount of transistors, with numbers surpassing billions on a single microchip, it is simply impossible to inspect everything on a given microprocessor. Consequently, commercial microchip manufacturers have to focus on assuring that the microprocessors perform the primary critical functions as defined by the original design. Any other circuitry embedded in the chip and not interfering with these critical functionalities will no be highlighted in any of the performance tests.   Furthermore, these tests will not be applied to all the thousands of microchips from the same batch, but rather to a selected few, since they are all considered identical. However, this is an assumption, not necessarily a proven fact.

Now, we have to considered the global manufacturing factor in our equation, since the semiconductor outsourcing movement dates back to the 1960s, when US microchip manufacturers transplanted the labor-intensive assembly and testing processes to locations mainly in Asia, offering less expensive labor workforces. Once this labor migration became an established fact, any adversary seeking to penetrate US government security can simply identify the type of microprocessors ordered by the US DoD and target them for malicious alterations. In cases where the microchip design becomes available, alterations can be introduced, resulting in microchips manufactured according to the original design, though with unauthorized embedded additional circuitry.[66]

There are primarily two avenues to disrupt or disable a processor. First, a kill switch represented by any malicious manipulation of either the software or hardware in the original design, with the intent of causing a fatal malfunction on the microchip. Second, a non-destructive alternative, by introducing a backdoor, allowing outsiders to obtain access to the system in order to disable or enable a particular functionality in the microchip. This second alternative maintain the unauthorized access obfuscated, keeping the

_____

http://spectrum.ieee.org/semiconductors/design/the-hunt-for-the-kill-switch
66   Ibid

victim unaware of the intrusion. For instance, a backdoor on the microprocessor operating a particular SDR (software-defined radio) or SDN (software-defined network) would disable or bypass battlefield radio encryption, sending all communications in clear text, with disastrous consequences for the victimized forces.

The introduction of a kill switch requires the addition of extra logic embedded into a microprocessor. This embedding can take place either during the design phase or the manufacturing process. An adversarial agent could introduce the spurious logic by simply substituting one of the masks used to imprint the pattern of wires and transistors onto the semiconductor wafer during the lithographic phase.

Defense contractors are heavily dependent on field-programmable gate arrays (FPGAs). This is a type of generic microchip manufactured as an integrated circuit designed to allow a designer or a customer the capability of configuring it after the manufacturing phase. The post-manufacturing configuration is accomplished via an array of programmable logic blocks. What is the problem? The majority of FPGAs are manufactured at foundries located outside the US.[67]

Any adversary seeking to penetrate US government security can simply identify the type of microprocessors ordered by the US DoD and target them for malicious alterations. In cases where the microchip design becomes available, alterations can be introduced, resulting in microchips manufactured according to the original design, though with unauthorized embedded additional circuitry.

The embedding of a kill switch would simply require the addition of about 1000 transistors, practically an insignificant

---

67 Ibid

amount among the billions of them on a modern microchip. These few additional transistors could then be programmed to respond to a very specific 512-bit instruction sequence. If these modified microprocessors find their way into routers supporting military networks, the trigger sequence would disable the microchip, with devastating consequences to national security. This type of attack would be very difficult to detect, and very easy to obfuscate.

Another scenario is the presence of either a kill switch or a backdoor built into an encryption microchip supporting secure communication equipment. This has the potential to cause even more disastrous consequences, since the encoding and decoding processes on secure communications depend completely on integrated circuitry. Accordingly, the presence of a kill switch or a backdoor would facilitate the disabling of the encoding process, resulting in unprotected messaging operations, detected and collected by an adversary.[68]

There is an abundance of technical papers available online addressing the concrete threats posed by counterfeits of integrated circuits (IC), including microprocessors, through the supply chain. The consequences can reach dramatic levels when critical or defense systems experience failure due to the use of defective counterfeit components.

The counterfeit category is broader than maliciously altered ICs. It also includes recycled, remarked, out-of-specs or defective, cloned, tampered IC components, and IC components with forged documentation. One of these technical and scholarly papers offers a comprehensive summary of all the available tests comprising the counterfeit detection methodology, including physical, electrical, and aging-based fingerprinting.[69]

Though these tests are effective in detecting counterfeit ICs,

---

68 Ibid
69 Guin, Ujjwal, et al. "Counterfeit Integrated Circuits: A Rising Threat in the Global Semiconductor Supply Chain." IEEExplore, Vol. 102, No. 8, August 2014. http://ieeexplore.ieee.org/stamp/stamp.jsp?arnumber=6856206

we must remember that the counterfeit issue remains a threat because of the sheer number of ICs that are received, but are not tested before deployment. This paper also outlines the dynamic interaction between the design, the foundry, and the assembly phases involved in the complex manufacturing and security processes comprising the creation of a microprocessor. This paper also reminds us of the ever-present threat of cloning during the manufacturing process, by creating an unauthorized an altered reproduction of the original chip design via reverse engineering.

The threat of reverse engineering a chip can be mitigated (but not eliminated) by introducing IC camouflaging technique, achieved by introducing dummy contacts into the layout of the chip design, confusing the attacker in correctly understanding the camouflaged logic gates, and misleading this adversary into an incorrect modified design.[70]

Counterfeit prevention and detection requires international standards. Currently, these standards address the problem of parts already circulating in the market. However, they address only certain types of counterfeits, and they do not develop avoidance mechanisms on counterfeit ICs.

There are many adverse circumstances surrounding the issue of developing innovative detection and avoidance solutions today, resulting in the inability to identify an IC component as counterfeit with a very high level of confidence. The ability to do so would require the performing of multiple test methods, given the great variety of different types of ICs. The chance of selecting a counterfeit component from a large lot is extremely small, and the test time and costs become major limiting factors.[71]

There are, however, successful developments in our fight against counterfeit cyber components. In 2010 the Department of Justice and Homeland Security announced 30 convictions of individuals involved in the illegal distribution of counterfeit network hardware manufactured in

---

70 Ibid
71 Ibid

China. The Operation Network Raider resulted in the seizure of more than 700 counterfeit Cisco network devices, representing an estimated retail value exceeding $140 millions. There are other individuals facing trial and some awaiting sentencing.[72]

One of the sentenced individuals is a Saudi citizen residing in Texas. He purchased counterfeit Cisco Gigabit converters, network modules designed to facilitate network interface upgrading, from an online vendor in China. His intention was to sell these modules to the US DoD for use by Marine Corps personnel operating in Iraq. The counterfeit modules were intended for use by the Marine Corps network transmitting troop movements and relaying intelligence data. This is a concrete case of premeditated cyber adversarial action against US forces. Another sentenced individual was a Chinese resident, convicted for trafficking in counterfeit Cisco products. He conducted his illegal activity while conducting business as a Chinese company, and then shipping the counterfeit devices to the US.

Counterfeit Cisco routers and switches manufactured in China represent a double threat: once installed in US military and government networks they offer the Chinese a backdoor into US secure communications, or a means to disrupt or disable secure US communications.[73]

Between 2007 and 2010, the US Immigration and Customs Enforcement (ICE) and the US Customs and Border Protection (CBP) seized 5.6 million counterfeit semiconductor devices intended for use in the aerospace, military, and communications sectors, among others. The

---

72 FBI. "Departments of Justice and Homeland Security Announce 30 Convictions, More Than $143 Million in Seizures from Initiative Targeting Traffickers in Counterfeit Network Hardware." FBI website, May 06, 2010. https://archives.fbi.gov/archives/news/pressrel/press-releases/departments-of-justice-and-homeland-security-announce-30-convictions-more-than-143-million-in-seizures-from-initiative-targeting-traffickers-in-counterfeit-network-hardware

73 Homeland Security Newswire. "Operation targeting counterfeit network hardware from China yield convictions, seizures." 12 May 2010. http://www.homelandsecuritynewswire.com/operation-targeting-counterfeit-network-hardware-china-yield-convictions-seizures

seized semiconductors were labeled with counterfeit trademarks from 87 North American, Asian and European semiconductor companies, and destined for importers in the US and other countries.[74]

We would do well in reminding ourselves that there is another dimension to the problems generated by the presence of counterfeits microprocessors within cyber systems operating in our defense and industrial sectors. The counterfeiters and the distributors of counterfeit cyber components obviously represent one dimension, while the other dimension is the naivety dimension represented by the users who place an implicit and undeserving degree of trust on microprocessors. Their faulty assumption is that microprocessors are not exposed to cyber attacks.

There is an enlightening professional paper advising us that we should not ascribe unquestionable trust to microprocessor hardware. Are we not aware that there is a global industry embedded in the whole chain of manufacturing microchips and other cyber components? Yes, we are aware. So where is the disconnect between this fact, and the implicit trust we place in the microprocessor? Such trust is completely misplaced, since microprocessor are exceedingly vulnerable to insider attacks throughout the entire manufacturing chain, crossing many international boundaries, and subject to the stratagems of many foreign entities participating in the global manufacturing chain. These vulnerabilities can seriously compromise the integrity, confidentiality and availability (ICA) status of cyber systems.[75]

---

74 FBI. "Departments of Justice and Homeland Security Announce 30 Convictions, More Than $143 Million in Seizures from Initiative Targeting Traffickers in Counterfeit Network Hardware." FBI website, May 06, 2010. https://archives.fbi.gov/archives/news/pressrel/press-releases/departments-of-justice-and-homeland-security-announce-30-convictions-more-than-143-million-in-seizures-from-initiative-targeting-traffickers-in-counterfeit-network-hardware

75 Waksman, A. & Sethumadhavan, S. "Tamper Evident Microprocessors." Columbia University, May 2010. http://web1.cs.columbia.edu/~simha/cal/pubs/pdfs/TEMP_Oakland10.pdf

Let us briefly expand on this premise of microprocessor untrustworthiness. During the different stages of the microchip development an adversary could alter the original design. During the hardware design, an adversary could introduce a backdoor in the original design, by embedding a few lines of code and modify an on-chip memory system to divert data items to a shadow address, in addition to the original address. This backdoor will compromise the ICA status of the cyber system depending on the compromised microchip, which will facilitate the extraction of sensitive data, the disabling of memory protections, and the shutting down of the cyber system according to an adversarial trigger. This scenario is beyond the theoretical level, reaching both military and public sectors.[76]

While it is unfeasible to test every single microchip deployed in a cyber system, we are not completely at the mercy of the counterfeiters. It is perfectly feasible, and highly advisable, to implement tailored tests on processors selected for critical cyber systems, in order to extract evidence leading to the detection of counterfeit microprocessors. This testing capability rests on the unavoidable indicators surfacing when the proper communications between microarchitectural subcomponents, built on a microprocessor, are disrupted by injected attacks on the microchip. The malicious actors may have succeeded in achieving the injection of malicious logic, but they cannot avoid the generation of detectable errors in the communication between the microarchitectural subcomponents in the microprocessor.

Microprocessor are exceedingly vulnerable to insider attacks throughout the entire manufacturing chain, crossing many international boundaries, and subject to the stratagems of many foreign entities participating in the global manufacturing chain. These vulnerabilities can seriously compromise the ICA status of cyber systems.

---

76 Ibid

Since all software is executed in and by a microprocessor, it follows that the root of trust on all cyber systems resides on the microprocessor. Since we should not "assume" that the processor is trustworthy, we shouldn't ascribe implicit trust to the cyber system depending on such microprocessor. The fact is that in the absence of a microprocessor trustworthiness series of tests, we should consider the cyber system built on such microprocessor as potentially compromised.

The foundation for the trustworthiness test on a microprocessor resides on the standard division of work between the different sub-components comprising a microprocessor. In addition to this, there are simple relationships that must exist between these sub-components.

Thus, the execution of any instruction executed by a microprocessor will consist of a series of separate but closely coordinated microarchitectural events. A memory instruction, for example, requires the use of a cache unit in addition to the use of the fetch, decode and register units. Any anomaly in the cooperation and coordination of this sub-components will provide indicators leading to the detection of microprocessor tampering, detectable by noticing alterations in the entire chain of events cause by an anomaly in one of the sub-components.

The age of innocence in computing no longer exist. We live in the age of contested computing, the age on untrusted computing.

Since the quest for total assurance on the trustworthiness of any given microprocessor is unattainable under normal circumstances, we should abandon the fallacious premise of ascribing implicit trust to any microprocessor, since it is the result of a global manufacturing process, involving many hands and agendas. Except in the case of critical systems, where me may afford to perform tailored and very expensive test on the underlying microprocessors, we have to contend with the fact that the rest of microprocessors performing in non-critical cyber systems remain an unknown cyber security factor. The alternate mitigating action is to remain alert, and monitor the behavior of the system. In the event of an anomaly representing a threat to the ICA status of the system in question, the investigation should include, whenever possible, the microprocessor itself.

Thus, the microprocessor represents the most important element in a cyber system, while at the same time representing the most significant unknown threat. Any private individual or enterprise should factor this reality in their risk management operational plan.

Chapter 6. From computer to NIC

All the data that has been processed by the microprocessor in our computers still remains in an isolated environment until we connect our computers to the network, and when we do so, a whole new scenario develops. The data we have created and processed in our cyber devices may have to travel from origin to destination. However, before the data initiates its travels, it would have to be formated in accordance to networking protocols. Furthermore, it will have to be translated into network language and structure.

In the same way that the keyboard represents the translator between the human user and the computer, likewise the network interface card (NIC) represents the translator between the computer and the network environment. As stated in the first chapter of this book, electronic computers do not communicate in any human language; they only "speak" binary language. So, now that the data produced and processed in the computer is ready to be sent through the networking path infrastructure, another translation process has to take place; the binary data has to be translated into networking language.

The NIC becomes the interface between the connected cyber device and the network infrastructure providing the networking service. The NIC has a very important role, since it is responsible for preparing, sending, and controlling the flow of data from the device into the network, and vice versa. We previously referred to the NIC as the other cyber translator, facilitating the translation of the binary language generated by the cyber device, into the language understood by the cabling system providing the networking service.

The NIC, therefore, has the task of translating the digital data format into electrical or optical signals, so the data can traverse the Internet's infrastructure. By participating in the global Internet, every NIC must have a unique identifier. A committee of the Institute of Electrical and Electronics

Engineers (IEEE) assigns blocks of addresses to each NIC manufacturer. They in turn place the unique identifying address into chips embedded on the NIC. Every manufactured NIC, therefore, comes with its own hardware address or MAC address, represented by 6 bytes (48 bits) in hexadecimal notation. The designator MAC is the acronym for Media Access Control.

The service of translation facilitated by the NIC is a very complicated process, but rendered transparently to the user of the cyber device. A connection to a desired web site starts with the user specifying the URL containing the domain name of the web site resource. In simplified terms, the cyber device passes the URL information to the NIC, which in turns translates the URL data into electrical pulses, when connecting to a traditional network cabling system, or optical signals in the case of fiber optic networking. Subsequently, the networking cables carry either the impulses or optic signals to the destination web server. When this web server replies with the requested data, the entire process is reversed. Either electrical impulses or optical signals will travel back to the requesting NIC, which will translate them into binary data understood by the cyber device originating the request. The corresponding browser will process the received data and will render it in visual format for the user.

There are two primary differences between a MAC address and an IP address: The former is a physical address, permanently associated with the NIC, while the latter is a logical address, not permanently associated with the NIC. When a cyber device connects to a different network, a new logical IP address is assigned to that cyber device. The MAC address of the NIC, however, remains unchanged (under normal circumstances).

There are several networking technologies available, but the most prevalent is the Ethernet technology. The entire formulation of networking technology is encapsulated in a theoretical concept known as the OSI Reference model, divided in seven layers. The layer number 1 is known as the physical layer (PHY), and is quite distinct from the other six layers. The PHY is responsible for interacting directly with the networking cabling infrastructure. This layer is TCP/IP incognizant. All the remaining six layers do interact with the TCP/IP set of protocols, in one form or another. The PHY does not, and it's the only layer where data transitions from a binary environment to a non-binary environment. All of the other six layers manipulate and prepare data to be sent to the networking environment, but they all depend on the PHY to transform the data into the format required by the networking environment.

Some of the responsibilities of the PHY include encoding and signaling (transforming binary data), and performing data transmission and reception. In the operational world of networking, the model of the TCP/IP set of protocols differs from the OSI model of networking. In this operational world the PHY layer is known as the network interface layer, or link layer. Why do we make this distinction? Because the OSI model is simply a theoretical reference model for networking. Given the universality of the predominant TCP/IP suite, the TCP/IP model performs the required functionalities outlined in the OSI model, but utilizing a consolidated practical model with only four layers, namely, application, transport, network, and link layer, the one where the NIC operates, in direct contact with the Ethernet networking environment.[77]

There is another very important function of the link layer. The TCP/IP suite can only identify a cyber system by its assigned logical IP address, which is correlated to the corresponding MAC address in the NIC. But when data is transferred via the networking environment, which is IP incognizant, how does the other networked node recognize its networked partner? During the data transfer on a network connection the NIC uses only the MAC address (the hardware address). When Ethernet traffic travels from origin to destination, the only identifiers for both the origin and destination are expressed in terms of the 48-bit hardware addresses, the MAC addresses. It is only this identifier that

77 Stevens, W. Richard. (1994) TCP/IP Illustrated, Volume 1. Addison Wesley.
      p 2

determines the destination interface. The logical IP addresses are not examined at this level, because this level does not "speak" TCP/IP, and does not understand the 32-bit IP logical address identifiers.

The NIC is the other cyber translator, facilitating the translation of the binary language generated by the cyber device, into the language understood by the cabling system providing the networking service.

This is the scenario at hand. We have two cyber systems connected to a network, namely, system Eros and system Venere. Eros prepares cyber data to send to Venere, but since the gateway into the network infrastructure is the NIC, and the NIC does not understand 32-bit IP logical addresses, but understands only 48-bit physical MAC addresses, how can the Eros NIC send the data to the Venere NIC?

This is the process taking place at the link layer. Eros prepares IP data packets containing a source and destination IP address encapsulated in the data packet. However, the Eros NIC cannot deliver the data because the Eros NIC does not know the Venere NIC MAC address. Remember, the NICs do not "speak" IP address language; they only "speak" MAC address language. In order to arrive at the Venere system, the data packet will have to be encapsulated into an Ethernet frame with a source and destination MAC address. Why? Because this is the language format of the link layer, responsible for delivering the network data into the Ethernet network environment.

Eros of course knows the source MAC address, which is its own. But how does Eros obtained Venere's MAC address? This is when we need the assistance of the Address Resolution Protocol (ARP). This protocol is designed to allow networked systems to communicate with each other. On an Ethernet network environment the two nodes attempting to connect must know each other's MAC address and their corresponding IP addresses. Only then these two nodes can communicate and transfer networked data between themselves.

Before Eros sends a datagram to Venere, it looks in its internal ARP table (cache) to ascertain if there is an entry in the cache for the MAC address and corresponding IP address for Venere. If such entry is missing in cache, Eros sends a broadcast message to every device on the network asking who in the common network has the destination IP address. This broadcast ARP message will reach every node in the common network, thus allowing all the networked devices to compare the broadcast IP address to its own. Only the node with the matching IP address will send an ARP reply to the source device, including its MAC address.[78] After receiving the ARP reply message, the source device adds the destination MAC address to its ARP table, for future reference. With this information Eros can prepare network data containing the destination MAC address for Venere, a required identifier for data traveling through the link layer. The figure below illustrates the ARP broadcast and response process.

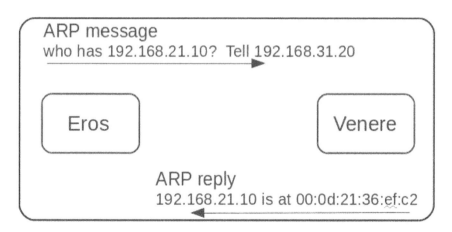

The message sent by Eros via the ARP request basically states "who has 192.168.21.10 and what is your MAC address?" Since Venere's MAC address is unknown, the

78 Cisco.com, Address resolution Protocol, 2012

broadcast ARP message is sent to destination MAC address FF:FF:FF:FF:FF:FF, which is everybody in the common network. Venere reply "I am the node with IP 192.168.21.10 and my MAC address is 00:0d:21:36:ef:c2. So, this little story about Eros and Venere, finding each other in the common network, and beginning to communicate in the Ethernet environment they share, seems to have a happy ending. Does it really?

Actually, we don't know with a 100% certainty if Venere is the node responding, simply because we may have a case of ARP spoofing in our hands, where a rogue answering system replies to the ARP request instead of Venere, with the goal of intercepting network data sent to Venere. The ever-present malicious user may use ARP spoofing to perform a man-in-the-middle (MITM) or denial-of-service (DoS) attack on the other users on the network.

How is this possible? Well, remember that the ARP request is broadcast to all the systems reachable in the common network by sending the ARP request to destination MAC address FF:FF:FF:FF:FF:FF (which is everybody). There are several software programs designed to detect and perform ARP spoofing attacks. After all, the ARP protocol does not provide protection against such attacks. Why? Because ARP was written in the age of innocence.[79]

The PHY is responsible for interacting directly with the networking cabling infrastructure, but this layer is TCP/IP incognizant. All the remaining six layers interact with the TCP/IP set of protocols, in one form or another. The PHY does not, and it's the only layer where data transitions from a binary environment to a non-binary environment. All of the other six layers manipulate and prepare data to be sent to the networking environment, but they all depend on the PHY to transform the data into the format

---

79   Giannelli, Lou. (2012) The Cyber Equalizer. Chapter 3. Xlibris Corporation

required by the networking environment.

Other than ARP spoofing, are there any other network dangers lurking in the cyber path? Of course. Did I mention packet sniffers before? Well, if I didn't, here it goes. When networked cyber devices talk to each other and exchange data over the network, there are ways to eavesdrop or "sniff" these exchanges. Sniffers were primarily designed for network administrators in assisting them with designing, studying, and troubleshooting networking issues. But once again, whatever humans invent for a positive goal can be misused for a malicious purpose, and this is the case of network sniffers. So, the problem is not on the creativity of the human mind, but on the propensity to evil in humankind.

A network sniffer is a software program capable of recording all network traffic on a particular network exchange session, presenting all the details and the data contained in the recorded network packets during a session. Sniffers are technically known under the term "network analyzers." There is a brief description and a sample of a network analyzer data available on a previous book by this author.[80]

Network analyzers act as the engines in network defensive programs known as Intrusion Detection Systems (IDS) and used by qualified and experienced cyber defenders to match packets against a known exploit signature, or to watch the prelude of an exploit attack before it becomes an intrusion. Of course, this defensive paradigm depends on cyber professionals operating on a proactive cyber defense posture, a very rare type of defense in our current age where automated network defenses are preferred, given the difficulty in gathering and employing truly qualified cyber defense subject matter experts (SMEs).[81]

The operation of a network analyzer requires specialized networking knowledge, because the analyzer does not provide answers; it simply provides undeniable network evidence of networked traffic. Only cyber professionals with

---

80 Ibid, pgs 39,40
81 Ibid, chapter 9

the required theoretical and empirical network knowledge can extract the answers from the gathered evidence.

The network analyzer works on the premise that cyber devices in a shared network environment have access to networked data broadcast to every node on the shared network segment (unless in a switched environment).[82] Therefore, the NIC on each node actually "sees" the data exchanged between the participating nodes, but ignores it, unless otherwise instructed. And this is the caveat upon which the network analyzer operates. What does it happen if we instruct the NIC to stop ignoring all the network traffic available on the shared network segment?

The network analyzer will instruct the NIC to enter into a promiscuous mode of operation, that is, to pay attention to all the network traffic available on the network wire, and capture and record the traffic data exchanged by all the nodes in the shared networked segment. This is equivalent to an individual being able to have access to all the communication exchange among neighbors in a residential area.

The traffic traversing the network wire comes in data packets, which a network analyzer is capable of peeling away the layers of encapsulation and decode the relevant information in the data packets, practically disclosing every piece of information exchanged between the nodes participating in the share network segment.[83]

So, now you can realize how a rogue user can collect the MAC address of neighboring nodes, and spoof them, along with the capability for launching a series of potentially damaging exploitation attacks. Do you have a house guest that connects to your home network? Do you know how much sensitive data that guest could potentially obtain from the members of your household? May I suggest something? Perhaps you may postpone your online banking while having

---

82 Symantec.com, Sniffers: What They Are and How to Protect Yourself, Matthew Tanase, February 26, 2002
83 Ibid

a house guest, just in case the guest uses a network analyzer (sniffer)? The rogue user doesn't have to share your roof; the threat may come from the residences surrounding your house, those within the reach of your Wi-Fi home router coverage area. Is your Wi-Fi router configured with the best available encryption? If you don't know, or if you simply bought and connected your Wi-Fi router without changing the default password and without configuring the best available encryption, then those withing reach of your Wi-Fi reach area may be using a network analyzer and collecting sensitive data from you.

Isn't this a rather extreme paranoid way of thinking? When it comes to protect your network data, a healthy degree of paranoia should be the standard. If someone parks inside the Wi-Fi range area of your home router, they can connect to your wireless router, become part of your wireless home network, and sniff all the network data, thus collecting sensitive personal and financial information from your household. When it comes to protect your network, the only safe level of defense is not to trust anyone.

Network analyzers act as the engines in network defensive programs known as Intrusion Detection Systems (IDS), provided they are used by qualified and experienced cyber defenders to match packets against a known exploit signature, or to watch the prelude of an exploit attack before it becomes an intrusion. This defensive paradigm depends on cyber professionals operating on a proactive cyber defense posture, a very rare type of defense in our current age where automated network defenses are preferred, given the difficulty in gathering and employing truly qualified cyber defense subject matter experts (SMEs).

One very important thing to remember is this: don't expect to have the perfectly secure network, because is an unattainable goal. Simply aspire to have a network more secure than others in your neighborhood.[84] Why? Because malicious actors usually seek the easier prey (unless you have concrete reasons to believe your represent a very specific target). Under normal circumstances a cyber predator looks for the less secure target, for targets of opportunity. If you represent a harder target in the area under attack, the cyber predator will discard you and continue searching for a weaker target.

The NIC, that wonderful device that allows us to network, may also be the port of entry for malicious users taking advantage of the less than secure configurations we may be using when joining a network with our cyber devices. Without the NIC our cyber devices remain isolated, but with the NIC, we are ushered into a whole world of networking opportunities, coexisting with a whole world of digital threats. We need to know how to secure the path we travel.

Now, since we all carry around those ubiquitous mobile cyber devices (smart phones, tablets, etc), they all come equipped with a wireless chipset that handles of your wireless network connectivity needs, and most of the time we carry them with their Wi-Fi settings on. So we may walk around a financial or commercial sector with our mobile devices on, but thinking we are going to be cautious and not try to connect to any unknown available Wi-Fi access point (AP). So, we should be safe under these cautious circumstances, right?

You may not attempt to connect to available APs as you traverse those sectors, but are you completely safe? No, you are not. How is it possible, if you are not connecting? You may not initiate any connections, but your Wi-Fi settings, which are on, are looking around for available APs, constantly scanning for them, and leaving a trail of all your movements. If you happen to be in London, your movement may be tracked by a set of networked trash containers strategically deployed in some commercial sections. Since those trash containers are designed to track the MAC

---

84 LinuxJournal.com, Packet Sniffing Basics, Adrian Hannah, Nov 14, 2011

address of every Wi-Fi enabled smart phone carried by people traversing the scanning area, during a one-week scanning period in June 2013, 12 trash containers tracked the location of over 4 million mobile devices withing the range of the scanning area. The captured data would allow for the mapping of the path followed by the devices' owners as they traverse the scanning area.[85]

Is your W-Fi router configured with the best available encryption? If you don't know, or if you simply bought and connected your Wi-Fi router without changing the default password and without configuring the best available encryption, then those withing reach of your Wi-Fi reach area may be using a network analyzer and collecting sensitive data from you.

One can only imagine the different scenarios deriving from the use (or abuse) of the metrics and analysis of the collected data, representing habits, behaviors, and preference of the owners of the scanned devices, who may lack complete situational awareness of this kind of tracking activity. What is the one important mitigation any user can implement to avoid this kind of unsolicited scanning and tracking? Turn your Wi-Fi setting off on your mobile device when you are not using it to purposely connect to a known and (reasonably) trusted AP. Otherwise, the MAC address in your mobile wireless device will disclose your location.

So, at this point I'd like to ask the reader: how is your piconet? You don't have one? That's strange, because currently just about everyone has and operates a piconet. Well, perhaps if a refrain my question, and ask: do you have interconnected Bluetooth devices in your residence? If the answer is yes, then you do have a piconet, the technical designation for a very small network of Bluetooth devices. Perhaps you have a Bluetooth printer that you use to print interesting articles you find when browsing from your smart

85 ArsTechnica.com, Smartphone-monitoring bins in London track places of
    work, past behavior, and more, Dan Goodin, Aug 9, 2013

phone. Or perhaps you have a stereo device connected to your smart phone music collection, or a Bluethooth stereo neckset you carry around for hands-free phone calls and for your music listening pleasure. This entire book was written using a piconet that connects my Linux system with my keyboard, my mouse, and my printer; all these devices interconnected without wires. Yes, piconets are ubiquitous, but this very same convenience represents a potential threat as well. There was an estimated three billion Bluetooth devices sold in 2014.

Why then did I ask about your piconet? Because we must not forget that Bluetooth is just another type of wireless technology available in our cyber devices. Bluetooth is the short-range radio frequency communication environment we use to implement wireless personal area networks (WPANs). This technology is deeply integrated into our daily routines because of the many provided conveniences, the least of which is the elimination of connectivity cables. The Bluetooth technology was originally developed in Scandinavia in 1994, and officially adopted in 1998. The Bluetooth Special Interest Group (SIG) is the non-profit organization that oversees the development of the Bluetooth standard.[86]

The security features on Bluetooth specifications require proper management. Failure to do so leaves users open to many security risks. One of the weakest security procedures occurs during the initial communication, or pairing. Every Bluetooth device is manufactured with a unique 48-bit identifier, the Bluetooth device address. This unique identifier is used as one of the factors to compute the link key, which is then transmitted in clear text, thus providing ample opportunity for a malicious cyber activity.[87]

It is the responsibility of the owner of the Bluetooth device to maintain a secure posture, simply because vendors issue Bluetooth devices with the Bluetooth radio turned on by default. Thus, these devices are continuously performing

---

86 https://www.bluetooth.org/en-us/members/about-sig
87 SANS Institute, Bluetooth And Its Inherent Security Issues, Tu C. Niem, 04 November 2002

inquiries to detect radio proximity with other Bluetooth devices. While in this inquiry condition, the Bluetooth device will disclose its unique identifier and clock status, since these components are required for pairing, and for calculating the link key used for communication between paired devices. The unique identifier and the clock status on the master Bluetooth device on a piconet are used to calculate the frequency hopping sequence required to establish communication with the piconet.

Bluetooth devices are typically deployed with a minimal security level, set by default as security mode 1. In this mode authentication and encryption are not required, thus enabling any Bluetooth device withing reach to connect and request data without the knowledge of the user on the other paired Bluetooth device. As the reader can see, these conditions represent a very unfavorable cyber security posture for the Bluetooth devices operating under this threat premise.[88]

The trust relationship established by two paired Bluetooth devices is persistent. Bluetooth devices in this trust relationship will keep the link keys in non-volatile memory, unless configured to delete them after a specified period of time. This condition becomes a threat risk in the case of a lost or stolen Bluetooth device previously paired. Other Bluetooth devices owned by the theft victim, and those of other users previously paired, are now exposed to unauthorized connections and eavesdropping. Why? Because the lost or stolen device already has the necessary authorization and authentication data to establish communications with the previously paired Bluetooth devices. The person in possession of the lost or stolen device doesn't have to do anything other than remain within the Bluetooth radio range in order to establish an unauthorized connection.[89]

Are there some simple precautions to mitigate the threat risk in Bluetooth devices? There are indeed a few; set your

---

88 Ibid
89 Ibid

Bluetooth device to the non-discoverable mode. Reactivate the discoverable mode only when a pairing operation is necessary, and set it back to the non-discoverable mode immediately after a successful pairing. This will prevent the Bluetooth device from responding to queries by unknown Bluetooth devices. During the pairing operation, conduct it in a private setting where you exercise some degree of control, to prevent attackers from intercepting the communication. The reader may consider consulting other available brief Bluetooth security guides.[90]

---

90 NSA Systems and Network Analysis Center, Bluetooth Security. A very detailed security guide is provided by NIST Special Publication 800-121 Revision 1, Guide to Bluetooth Security, June 2012

Chapter 7. The Wi-Fi Residential Router

Let us pause for a moment to examine the one device providing us with the Wi-Fi connectivity in our own residence. In the previous chapter we spoke about the NIC, and AP, and Wi-Fi, but how is it that all those networks connectivity items come together in our residential wireless local area network (WLAN)?

Enter the Wi-Fi router, the focal point of any WLAN, the device that generates the Wi-Fi signals allowing cyber systems to joint the WLAN, and establish an Internet connection. There are several cyber security concerns we have to consider when operating a residential Wi-Fi router.

Before entering into the technical details of the Wi-Fi router, let us consider the importance of this device, and the implications of making wise choices when purchasing and operating this important wireless device. After all, this is the one device that either will protect us from cyber attacks, or the instrument of our network security doom. Let us then begin with an analogy.

When you purchase your current car, did you take the ignition key from the dealer, walk to your brand new car, and sped away within the first 20 seconds after taking position at the driver's seat? Of course not! You certainly took your time to familiarize yourself with the different controls of your new car, made a number of adjustments (seat, mirrors, etc), and then you carefully drove away in order to adjust yourself to the new driving conditions (front, lateral, rear visibility factors), and the driving characteristics of your brand new car.

Well, getting a new residential Wi-Fi router should follow a similar adjustment and configuration process. You do NOT take the Wi-Fi router our of the box, plug it in, power it on, and immediately connect to the Internet! You need to learn the settings of your new Wi-Fi router, proceed carefully through the initial configuration process, apply all the secure necessary settings required to protect your residential WLAN, save the new settings, check once again that you applied the required setting for your cyber protection, and then, and ONLY then, you connect to the Internet. Why? Because cyber attackers are waiting for the myriad of naive users doing exactly what I just told you NOT to do. I do not have either the time or the space to tell you about all the disastrous cases of users who fail to take these precautions, and became another number of the continually growing cyber statistical preys that trusted the default settings out of the box on a residential router.

Very important. Prior to buying your residential Wi-Fi router, seek the advice of a trustworthy and knowledgeable person who can assist you in buying a router equipped with the proper security capabilities, and buy it from a reputable manufacturer.[91] Select a router offering Wi-Fi Protected Access 2 (WPA2)-Advanced Encryption Standard (AES), and reject any routers supporting only the vulnerable Wired Equivalent Privacy (WEP). WPA2-AES encrypts the communication between the wireless router and the wireless computing device, providing stronger authentication and authorization between the devices, incorporating the AES 128-bit encryption. The selection of WPA2-AES is encouraged by the National Institute of Standards and Technology (NIST).[92]

The residential or corporate wireless router is the most important link between the user(s) and the WWW, so it has a highly privileged position that hackers can exploit. Regretfully, many such routers are manufactured with insecure default configurations, contain back-door accounts, expose legacy services and have unsecured firmware.

The sad reality is that residential router software is designed with a utilitarian goal, and not necessarily with network

---

91 Some disreputable manufacturers are mention later in this chapter.
92 US-CERT. "Security Tip (ST15-002) Securing Your Home Network." December 16, 2015. https://www.us-cert.gov/ncas/tips/ST15-002

security in mind. When it comes to routers provided by ISPs, the scenario is even more ominous, since they are quite possibly configured in a rather insecure way, or perhaps configured in a manner that offers the ISP a monitoring capability. Residential cyber products are always subject to the marketing factor, requiring software developed as inexpensively as possible, since functionality, not cyber security, is the leading priority.[93]

For this reason, one of the most important decision in protecting your residential Wi-Fi network is to avoid using routers supplied by ISPs. They also have additional disadvantages when compared to those available directly from manufacturers. ISP-provided residential routers are less secure, and designed with embedded hard-coded remote support credentials provided by the ISP. Users are not allowed to modify or eliminate these remote credentials. This creates a very invasive environment. Furthermore, the patches for the ISP customized firmware versions usually lag behind security patches for the same flaws released by router manufacturers.[94]

You do NOT take the Wi-Fi router our of the box, plug it in, power it on, and immediately connect to the Internet! You need to learn the settings of your new Wi-Fi router, proceed carefully through the initial configuration process, apply all the secure necessary settings required to protect your residential WLAN, save the new settings, check once again that you applied the required setting for your cyber protection, and then, and ONLY then, you connect to the Internet.

---

93 Horowitz, Michael. "Router Bugs Flaws Hacks and Vulnerabilities." Router Security, October 20, 2016
October 20, 2016. http://routersecurity.org/bugs.php
94 Constantin, Lucian. "How to secure your router and home network." IDG News Service, Jul 8, 2016.
http://www.csoonline.com/article/3093385/security/how-to-secure-your-router-and-home-network.html

Acquiring a Wi-Fi router is more than just obtaining the privilege of achieving Internet connectivity; it is a also acquiring the responsibility to manage the Wi-Fi device, because it represents the power to control and determine who and what is granted access into our residential cyber kingdom. Your WLAN is your sovereign domain, so treat it as such, and exercise the right to determine who and what is allow to come in, and who and what is allowed to go out of your cyber kingdom.

Regretfully, many users do not exercise this power, and neglect the Wi-Fi router into oblivion, by relinquishing the power of controlling the residential WLAN, and abdicating the right to monitoring the one device containing all the information related to the inbound and outbound network traffic. Even worse, when falling prey to a cyber attack, they don't even know how and who invaded their cyber kingdom, and they surrender to their defeat. How have we come to willingly adopt this attitude of passive surrender?

The first action upon purchasing a Wi-Fi router from a reputable manufacturer is to change the default administrator password. It is your router and you, and only you, should have complete control on the Wi-Fi router. The cyber criminal world has extensive lists of the default administrator passwords used by manufacturers, and attackers constantly attempt to try these default passwords to infiltrate private WLANs.

ISP-provided residential routers are less secure, and designed with embedded hard-coded remote support credentials provided by the ISP. Users are not allowed to modify or eliminate these remote credentials, thus creating an invasive environment. Furthermore, the patches for the ISP customized firmware versions usually lag behind security patches for the same flaws released by router manufacturers.

Avoid purchasing Wi-Fi routers associated with foreign

companies maintaining an affiliation with foreign nations harboring an adversarial attitude against the USA. Such manufacturers go to great extremes to infiltrate the supply chain into USA with tampered Wi-Fi devices. There are several official US governments reports exposing these adversarial entities, targeting the US government and the US society. One such report highlights the fact that a research on the issue of counterfeited electronic components, flooding the US market, reveals that more than 70 percent of them originate in China.[95] Counterfeit in electronic devices is only part of the problem; such devices serve an additional purpose in facilitating the activity represented by the foreign intelligence entity (FIE) threat.

A 2016 report published by the Office of the Director of National Intelligence (ODNI) states that in response to the FIE threat the US has launched a strategy to disrupt it, along with the actions of cyber intruders, and international industrial competitors with ties to these entities. Their combined nefarious activities include overt, covert, and clandestine methods to compromise our national security. The objectives for this US strategy include disruption of cyber exploitations linked to these FIEs.[96]

Very recently, in September 2016, we witnessed a large DDoS attack launched by a botnet comprised largely of over 11,000 residential compromised routers. They were manufactured by eight different vendors, with the largest percentage represented by the Chinese exploited Huawei-based routers, and the BHU Wi-Fi router, another Chinese vendor. This router is accessible from the Internet, facilitates an easy escalation of privileges from admin to root, and it enables SSH at startup, in addition to offering a hard-coded root password.[97] These factory configuration settings, quite

---

95 Report 112–167 of the COMMITTEE ON ARMED SERVICES UNITED STATES SENATE. May 21, 2012. https://www.gpo.gov/fdsys/pkg/CRPT-112srpt167/pdf/CRPT-112srpt167.pdf

96 Office of the Director of National Intelligence. National Counterintelligence Strategy of the United States of America 2016. https://www.ncsc.gov/publications/strategy/docs/National_CI_Strategy_2016.pdf

97 Horowitz, Michael. "Router Bugs Flaws Hacks and Vulnerabilities." Router

possibly by design, greatly facilitate cyber intrusions into residential or corporate networks. Chinese ZTE routers are also very vulnerable to malware targeting specific flaws in them. It's feasible to extrapolate that such flaws are also present by design.

The scale of this DDoS, launched from a botnet comprised of residential routers, is quite unprecedented. These compromised routers represented 25% of the IP addresses utilized during the DDoS attack, with the largest number of them from Huawei routers, including versions HG8245H, HG658d, HG531, etc. Other devices included NuCom 11N Wireless Routers, Dell SonicWalls, VodaFone, Netgear, and Cisco-IOS routers. This DDoS attack exhibited another interesting characteristic; the vast geographical distribution represented by autonomous systems (ASN), ISPs and IP addresses. The geographical distribution for this residential router botnet included devices in North, Central and South Americas, Caribbean, and Europe.[98]

Avoid purchasing Wi-Fi routers associated with foreign companies maintaining an affiliation with foreign nations harboring an adversarial attitude against the USA. Such manufacturers go to great extremes to infiltrate the supply chain into USA with tampered Wi-Fi devices.

So, what is it that a cautious and alert user can do to contribute to the goal of denying these adversaries the opportunity to harm our country's cyber security, including our own residential security? The proper course of action is to establish a responsible and proactive management of our residential WLAN. Am I hyperbolizing the importance of residential WLAN security? Absolutely not. The consequences of not doing so should be still fresh in our collective minds, from a recent and significant DDoS event.

Security, October 20, 2016
October 20, 2016. http://routersecurity.org/bugs.php

98 Cid, Daniel. "IoT Home Router Botnet Leveraged in Large DDoS Attack." Securi, September 1, 2016. https://blog.sucuri.net/2016/09/iot-home-router-botnet-leveraged-in-large-ddos-attack.html

Excursus: The Dyn DDoS

Less than a week ago[99] the Mirai botnet was unleashed and became the primary source of a Distributed Denial of Service (DDoS) attack, disrupting the Managed DNS infrastructure operated by Dyn. The impact of this cyber attack disrupted services during two separate time windows: from 11:10 to 13:20 UTC, and from 15:50 until 17:00 UTC.[100]

The malicious attack was very dynamic, and changed strategy in response to the defensive protocols launched by Dyn. During the defensive measures Dyn observed the disrupting traffic was originating from a very large group of IP addresses from all global geographical areas. This vicious and unprecedented type of attack highlights the pervasive cyber vulnerabilities of "Internet of Things" (IoT) devices, that became the primary cyber slaves controlled by the malicious botnet orchestrating the attack against Dyn.

The Mirai IoT botnet, active since 2016, operates on a large collection of exploited Internet-enabled DVRs, surveillance cameras, and other Internet-enabled devices. This high-impact DDoS botnet serves as the basis for a DDoS-for-hire 'booter'/'stresser' service, allowing attackers to disrupt the services of a target of their choice. This recent attack was directed against Dyn infrastructure, with the Mirai botnet encompassing a floating population of approximately 500,000 compromised IoT devices worldwide, with high concentrations of exploited devices in China, Hong Kong, Macau, Vietnam, Taiwan, South Korea, Thailand, Indonesia, Brazil, and Spain. Additional concentrations have also been observed in North America, Europe, and Oceania.[101]

---

99 This section was written on 26 October 2016

100 Hilton, Scott. "Dyn Analysis Summary Of Friday October 21 Attack." Dyn.com, October 26, 2016. http://hub.dyn.com/dyn-blog/dyn-analysis-summary-of-friday-october-21-attack

101 Dobbins, R., & Bjarnason S. "Mirai IoT Botnet Description and DDoS Attack Mitigation." ArborNetworks.com. 10/26/2016. https://www.arbornetworks.com/blog/asert/mirai-iot-botnet-description-

Dyn is a very important provider of core Internet services, including the essential DNS service, to many large organizations. The impact that millions of IoT devices had on Dyn infrastructure affected users across the globe. Were the owners of these IoT devices aware of their role in contributing to this widespread interruption of Internet services? Were they aware that their IoT devices had been recruited by malicious actors seeking to utilize these devices as the throng of infected bots causing the disruption? Very likely not. However, let's not dismiss this issue too quickly. Is lack of awareness a factor in determining the responsibility of an action?

Let's take this argument into the environment of an analogy borrowed from the traffic laws. If a driver causes harm to another individual, but this driver raises the argument of not being aware of causing harm to someone else, is this driver legally exonerated from liability?

If a user owns and operates IoT devices, such user is responsible for the activity and consequences of operating such devices. If such user made no attempt to secure the IoT devices from becoming victims of cyber exploits, the responsibility for the harm caused to other cyber devices belongs to the owner of the IoT devices causing the harm.

Cyber security researchers have discovered that the vulnerable embedded systems, such as the ones participating in the Dyn DDoS attack, are typically listening on inbound telnet access on TCP/23 and TCP/2323 ports. They also discovered that given the prevalence of continuous scanning for vulnerable nodes, the time to compromise a vulnerable IoT device is 10 minutes or less, unless the owner of these IoT devices take proactive steps to prevent access on ports TCP/23 and TCP/2323 to the targeted devices.[102] That of course requires for the owner of these devices to keep a vigilant monitoring eye on the residential router, and actively deactivate access to these

---

ddos-attack-mitigation/
102 Ibid

highly vulnerable ports.

If a user of IoT devices does not monitor the behavior of these devices while connected to the Internet, it is quite possible such devices are already part of a botnet, and therefore, are contributing to the disruption of critical services, affecting other users around the world.

In response to the role of so many compromised IoT devices participating in the disruption of Internet services via the Mirai botnet, a very typical approach has already surfaced. It advocates for the convenient and irresponsible "pass the buck" approach. This approach proposes a way to deflect the responsibility to someone else. If your IoT device is participating on the Mirai botnet, because as the owner you fail to protect this device, then let's propose that your ISP should be the one to assume the responsibility of controlling and protecting your IoT devices.[103]

In addition to being irresponsible, these approach is also ludicrous. What possible motivation would your ISP have to assume this additional responsibility? Are you prepared to pay for this extra protection? Is your ISP even willing to assume this additional task? Furthermore, and recalling on our recent analogy, are you considering to take the same approach with your personal vehicle, and expect the dealer to assume the responsibility for damages you caused while failing to control your car? If a user decides to acquire IoT devices, that very same user is responsible for the activities generated by such devices. That is the bottom line. Ownership comes with responsibility.

A final reminder at the time of closing this excursus; once an IoT device has become a cyber slave to the Mirai botnet, it immediately begins scanning for other vulnerable devices to compromise. The owner of these compromised devices, now attacking other devices, is liable for the harm caused to

---

103 Newman, Lily. "Internet Providers Could Be the Key to Securing All the IoT Devices Already out There." Wired.com, October 27, 2016. https://www.wired.com/2016/10/internet-providers-key-securing-iot-devices-already/

other people and other systems. Let us exercise responsible ownership, and assume the responsibility of securely managing the cyber devices we own; the tools are already available in your residential router.

In response to the role of so many compromised IoT devices participating in the disruption of Internet services via the Mirai botnet, a very typical approach has already surfaced. It advocates for the convenient and irresponsible "pass the buck" approach.

Let's resume then the topic of securely configuring our residential Wi-Fi router. We must make sure that the web-based management interface of the router is not reachable from the Internet, but rather from a private IP address under the owner's control. It is extremely rare when there is a truly justified reason to manage the router from outside the residential WLAN. When such is the case, the owner should have an above average knowledge of remote connectivity, and the technical skills to do so securely. The preferred methodology to enable remote management to the residential Wi-Fi router should take place via a VPN (virtual private network) solution.[104] This arrangement contributes to establishing a secure channel to the residential WLAN, and once on a secure channel, the owner can proceed to access the router's management interface.

A mature network security minded user should also restrict which unique private IP address can manage the Wi-Fi router, even when such management is conducted inside the WLAN. This unique private IP address should not be available from the pool of IP addresses assigned to the residential networked devices via DHCP (Dynamic Host Configuration Protocol).

---

104 Constantin, Lucian. "How to secure your router and home network." IDG News Service, Jul 8, 2016.
http://www.csoonline.com/article/3093385/security/how-to-secure-your-router-and-home-network.html

When connecting to the Wi-Fi router interface, turn on HTTPS access (if available), and always log out and close the management session when the task is completed. Use the browser in incognito or private mode when interacting with the Wi-Fi router management interface, in order to avoid leaving behind cookies from the management session. Never allow the browser to save the router's user name and password.[105] This is a precaution to avoid granting a visitor or a member of the family in your residence access to the router management interface. If they use your computer and browser, they could potentially reestablish a management session to your Wi-Fi router, and modify the router's settings without your consent.

Enable a complex Wi-Fi password and the strongest available security protocol on your residential router. WPA2 (Wi-Fi Protected Access II) should be the best option at the present. Avoid selecting the older WPA and WEP which are susceptible to brute-force attacks. If the router offers the option, create a guest wireless network, also protected with WPA2 and a strong password. Let visitors or friends use this isolated guest network instead of your main one. They might not have malicious intentions, but their devices might be compromised or infected with malware.

Exercise strict control on the number of network services your router exposes to the internet. The rule of thumb? Open only the services you need to conduct your businesses. Check for the services already open, check with the few ones you really need, and shut down all others; the fewer, the better. Avoid at all cost to leave open services like Telnet, UPnP (Universal Plug and Play), SSH (Secure Shell), and HNAP (Home Network Administration Protocol). They should not be reachable from the internet, because they represent serious security risks.[106]

Having a residential Wi-Fi router is not just a privilege; it's also a duty, which involves keeping your router's firmware up to date. This is done by regularly checking the

---

105 Ibid
106 Ibid

manufacturer's support website for firmware updates. Locate you particular router model, locate the corresponding firmware update, and follow the instructions offered by the manufacturer's website. Make absolutely certain that no one in your residence is attempting to connect to your Wi-Fi router during the firmware update operation.

If you prefer to operate IoT devices in your WLAN, consider network segmentation to isolate them, because they are risky devices. Some consumer routers offer the option to create VLANs (virtual local area networks) inside a private WLAN. These virtual networks can be used to isolate the IoT devices, usually rushed into marketing and containing a great deal of vulnerabilities. IoT devices often expose unprotected administrative protocols to the local network, and an attacker could easily break into such a device from a compromised computer, connected to the same network.

For the second consecutive year DEFCON 24 held the IoT Village dedicated to assess the cyber security status of IoT devices through a series of workshops dedicated to target the numerous vulnerabilities of these type of devices. There were over a 100 critical vulnerabilities discovered among the assessed off-the-shelf IoT devices, highlighting the endemic problem of IoT manufacturers disregarding the cyber security problems embedded in their products.[107]

Residential routers offer an additional security layer via MAC address filtering. By enabling MAC address filtering the security minded owner can deny rogue devices access into the protected residential Wi-Fi network. This cyber protection methodology is very effective, enabling the router's owner to restrict which devices are allowed on the Wi-Fi network, based on their MAC address.[108] This is the unique identifier on each cyber device equipped with a physical network card. Enabling this feature can prevent attackers from connecting to a Wi-Fi network even if they had previously stolen its

107 The author personally attended Black Hat and DEFCON 24 in August 2016
108 Constantin, Lucian. "How to secure your router and home network." IDG News Service, Jul 8, 2016.
http://www.csoonline.com/article/3093385/security/how-to-secure-your-router-and-home-network.html

password.

When connecting to the Wi-Fi router interface, use the browser in incognito or private mode, in order to avoid leaving behind cookies from the management session. Never allow the browser to save the router's user name and password.

This entire section about residential routers is dedicated to provide residential and corporate owners with a degree of situational awareness based on concrete information on the status of Wi-Fi routers. They are a necessary tool, but they are subject to many vulnerabilities, either by design or by omission. The marketing of these devices requires certain compromises between profit, functionality, and security, with the latter assigned the lowest priority. It remains the responsibility of the owner of these devices to implement the appropriate configuration settings in order to mitigate the risk of a cyber attack.

Chapter 8. Ready for take off

Now that we covered the cyber security issues related to the NIC and residential routers, we should be ready to take off and begin our Internet adventures, right? Or have we really covered the entire scope of how to gain access to Internet connectivity? The answer is no. The NIC grants you the capability of networking, and the Wi-Fi router grants you the capability of generating a residential wireless LAN. However, these capabilities remain dormant until you obtain a residential gateway into the Internet, and in order to achieve this step there is a critical missing device, the modem. Once your router connects to a modem with an active network signal, then and only then you'll be able to obtain Internet connectivity. Your Wi-Fi router is simply the first cyber device, inside your residence, connected to the real gateway, the modem.

Just as we advised the readers in the previous chapter to consider avoiding the use of an ISP-provided Wi-Fi router, the same advice is relevant when it comes to modems. Yes, I know how convenient is to simply establish a service contract with your local ISP and have them to bring the Internet signal through a coaxial cable into your residential environment, and connect this coaxial cable to an ISP-provided modem. Then you will have to go through the configuration process with your ISP, and finally receive the network connection signal that will open the gateway for you to obtain Internet connectivity.

However, before you get too excited about joining the Internet village, pause for a moment and think: do you want to consider what is best for your residential cyber security? Are you simply looking for the convenience of connectivity without any regard for cyber security, or would you rather choose the convenience of the Internet connectivity service plus maintaining personal control on your residential cyber security status? This decision will determine the type of modem you select to joint the Internet village. Accordingly, you should make this decision before contacting your local ISP for a contract service on Internet connectivity. The following graphic offers a simplified concept of a residential network.

The cyber security issue to consider depends on the amount of control the residential user has over the modem. If the option of an ISP-provided modem is the choice, the user will have no control over the performance and security of the device, and will have to pay an extra monthly fee for the use of the modem. Essentially, this user is paying an additional monthly fee, while having absolutely no control over the ISP-provided modem. If the residential user decides to purchase a commercially available modem, compatible with the local IPS guidelines, then this user will have full control on the quality of service, cyber security, and performance of the modem, plus full control on the configuration of the modem, and no additional monthly fee.

In general, local ISPs limit access to the Web-based control interface of rental modems, thus leaving the user without access to monitor or to modify network settings in order to obtain better performance or enhance cyber security. Users should also consider that the pool of available modems provided by a local ISP may be older models, and very likely previously used by former customers of the same local ISP.

By purchasing a newer and better commercially available modem, with support for new Internet technologies supported by the local ISP, the user retains control over the configuration settings and management of the modem. Additionally, if the user subscribes to a high-speed package offered by the ISP, the newer modem will provide this user with a better performance. Ownership of our modem allows us to have full access to the management interface, and be able to monitor traffic logs, signal quality, or troubleshoot connectivity issues.[109]

If the reader wants to consider the alternative of modem ownership, the terminology can be a little bit confusing. So far we have referred to the modem as the true gateway, meaning, the modem is the one single device that connects your residence to the Internet, through the middleman, your local ISP. However, in the advertising business, vendors are less specific when it comes to technical terms, and they used the term gateway to designate a hybrid device, combining both the router and the modem functionalities. Vendors may refer to this mixed device as either a router-modem combo, or sometimes they used the terminology wireless residential gateway. The modem, whether by itself, or in combination with a router, is always the gateway connecting your residence with your local ISP.

The residential modem is a device with a longer history that a residential Wi-Fi router. The modem dates back to the 1960s, as a device designed to allow connecting terminals to

109 Geier, Eric. "Ditch your ISP's modem and change your Internet experience forever." PCWorld, Oct 21, 2013.
http://www.pcworld.com/article/2056140/ditch-your-isps-modem-and-change-your-internet-experience-forever.html

a remote computer over the phone lines. The term modem is actually a contraction of the terms modulator-demodulator, thus modem. This device is responsible for taking computer digital data on the sending side, and modulate it into a signal compatible with the phone line data format. Then, the reverse process is completed at the receiving side, by another modem responsible for demodulating the signal and formatting it as digital data again.

When a residential user decides to purchase a commercially available modem, compatible with the local IPS guidelines, but declining an ISP-provided modem, then this user will have full control on the quality of service, cyber security, and performance of the modem, plus full control on the configuration of the modem, and no additional monthly fee.

Today, however, the Internet connectivity technology uses the cable TV media instead of the phone line. Through the cable TV our local ISP can offer a high-speed connection through the single coaxial cable provided by your ISP into the outlet in your wall, as illustrated in the graphic above. So, let's return to the issue we left pending, that is, the readers' resolution on whether to select a residential modem as a single device, or a combination modem-router device.

The first thing to consider is the technologies associated with these two connectivity devices. The modem technology is very stable and doesn't experience a great deal of changes. The residential router, on the other hand, depends on technology that changes and improves quite frequently. This condition points to an important decision factor: if one device experiences changes very rarely, and the other quite frequently, is it a good idea to combine them? Maintaining a set of these two devices as separate units will certainly facilitate the upgrade of the one changing more frequently, without the expense of upgrading an entire combo set when the modem component has experienced no change. Besides, the combo sets are always more expensive than the two separate components.

When it comes to maintaining control on the configuration and settings of both the modem and the router, it is always preferable to have two separate components. The combo set, due to the intricacies of combining both modem and router in one, offers limited access and less control. By comparison, a dedicated modem and a dedicated router always offer the owner more control and settings, and firmware upgrades.

There is one current modem technology the reader should consider in order to obtain the best available performance. If the user is connecting through coaxial cable TV, and researching through the commercially available modem models, the user may opt for using the latest specification represented by the DOCSIS standard supported by the available modern modem models.

The Data Over Cable Service Interface Specification (DOCSIS) is an international standard, functioning as a Point to Multipoint communications system, and designed for high-bandwidth data transfer through the cable TV media. This international standard includes contributions from operators and vendors from North and South America, Europe and Asia, and allows ISPs to implement and offer their local clients with an Internet access service. The ISPs can simply use the cable infrastructure already in place in the service area, either as an all-coax or hybrid-fiber-coax (HFC) network in their area of operation, and make this high-bandwidth Internet connectivity available to their local clients.[110]

----

110 Detailed technical specifications are readily available. Cable Television Laboratories, Inc. "Data-Over-Cable Service Interface Specifications. CM-TR-MGMTv3.0-DIFF-V01-071228." CableLabs, December 28, 2007, https://www.cablelabs.com/wp-content/uploads/specdocs/CM-TR-MGMTv3.0-DIFF-V01-071228.pdf, and Cable Television Laboratories, Inc. "Data-Cable Service Interface Specifications DOCSIS 3.1. MAC and Upper Layer Protocols Interface Specification. CM-SP-MULPIv3.1-I01-131029." CableLabs, October 29, 2013. https://www.cablelabs.com/wp-content/uploads/specdocs/CM-SP-MULPIv3.1-I01-131029.pdf

Since its release in 1997, DOCSIS has undergone several iterations. The latest standard is DOCSIS 3.1, released in October 2013. DOCSIS 3.0 brought an increase in data rates, both upstream and downstream, and introduced support for the more secure IPv6. DOCSIS 3.1 brought an additional increase ranging from 10 Gbit/s downstream and 1 Gbit/s upstream. If the reader considers the acquisition of a modern modem equipped with the DOCSIS 3.1 standard, Is prudent to consult with the local ISP, and present the question if they support DOCSIS 3.1 to the technical support personnel. Make sure the question is posed to ISP technical personnel, not to the the call center personnel. These individuals may not be aware of the nuances of backward compatibility between DOCSIS 3.1 and 3.0

Currently there is some debate on whether this backward compatibility issue is guaranteed. Consequently, it is prudent to present this question to qualified ISP technical personnel well informed on the DOCSIS 3.1 standard. CableLabs does emphatically states in their web site that "DOCSIS 3.1 devices are backwards compatible and will operate on a DOCSIS 3.0 system."[111]

After considering the alternatives between renting or owning a modem, and whether to use a separate or a combo device, we still have to face the responsibility of securing the cyber status of our modem. There are neither perfect modems nor perfect routers, so the cyber security issue is a recurrent issue. The popularity of certain modems, as advertised by enthusiastic reviewers, should not me misconstrued as a guarantee of their security standing. Most recommendations are based on features and functionality, not necessarily on cyber security standards.

Let's take for instance the recent case of a critically acclaimed modem, that after several endorsements was exposed in 2016 as being vulnerable to a cyber security flaw that could totally disable Internet access for those using such previously acclaimed modem. The flaw allows an unauthorized person to access the hard-coded

---

111 http://www.cablelabs.com/innovations/featured-technology/

administrative interface and execute a restart command, thus disabling the modem, and terminating the Internet connectivity for the affected owner.

Now, this is the lesser problem. The bigger problem occurs when the same unauthorized person decides to execute a command to reset all the default options, and restore the factory configuration to the modem, thus deleting all the settings implemented by the local ISP. Now the owner is not only completely disconnected from the local ISP, but the modem has been rendered unusable, since all the settings required to connect to the ISP have been deleted.[112]

In 2015 there was an even more ominous problem with Huawei 4G USB modems, affected by remote execution and denial of service vulnerabilities. This vulnerability not only affects the modem, but could allow attackers to hijack the computers connected to the affected modem.[113]

There are neither perfect modems nor perfect routers, so the cyber security issue is a recurrent issue. The popularity of certain modems, as advertised by enthusiastic reviewers, should not me misconstrued as a guarantee of their security standing. Most recommendations are based on features and functionality, not necessarily on cyber security standards.

The information in this chapter is to provide the reader with the require knowledge on the cyber security issues emanating from the use of connectivity devices we tend to accept and trust implicitly. This information is designed to

112 Casey, Henry. "Millions of Cable Modems Vulnerable to Easy Attack." Tom's Guide, Apr 8, 2016. http://www.tomsguide.com/us/arris-surfboard-cable-modem-vulnerable,news-22522.html

113 Pauli, Darren. "Remote code exec hijack hole found in Huawei 4G USB modems." The Register, 7 Oct 2015. http://www.theregister.co.uk/2015/10/07/remote_code_exec_hijack_hole_found_in_huawei_4g_usb_modems/

provide the reader with a broader and deeper understanding on the cyber security issues associated with residential routers and modems.

The bottom line? These two devices are neither secure nor trustworthy, and they cannot be trusted implicitly. These two types of devices can expose our residential networks and data to malicious attacks. The goal for the reader? To be cautiously aware of the threats, and to responsibly monitor both the inbound and outbound digital traffic passing through these devices. We should remain in control of them, and protect the cyber security status of our private cyber data.

Chapter 9. The unseen collector

In the preceding chapters we covered the work of the NIC, that wonderful device that allows us to connect to a network, and interact with other networks. So, now that you are connected, you want to explore the plethora of data available on the World Wide Web (WWW). What would you say if I told you that the data that defines your activities and preferences, your personality, idiosyncrasies and habits on line is being collected, threatening your privacy?

Consequently, we need to talk about yet another path that data generated at your cyber device will traverse. Is this another path formed by a very expensive cyber infrastructure that carries your data from origin to destination, different than the other paths covered in this book? The answer is no. This path travels the same general cyber infrastructure, but leads to an interactive methodology, whereby you post a query related to a topic of your interest, and in return you received a series of alternative answers, with a different degree of relevance to your original query. Yes, you guessed it correctly: we are referring to the web search engine.

In popular parlance people tend to refer to it as an Internet search engine, but this is a misnomer. The search engines we regularly use operate withing the context of the WWW, and the WWW is only a subset of the Internet. The proper name is the WWW search engine, because the search is limited only to WWW content, hosted on web servers. The conglomerate of global web servers is hosted on the Internet infrastructure, but this conglomerate is only a portion of the Internet infrastructure.

Today you can search the WWW for a very broad list of topics or keywords, and receive a myriad of sources referring you to web sites with content germane to the desired topic. What you can do today is not the same as it was a couple of decades ago. Back then you had to perform a very specific and accurate search query in order to obtain the desired results. Today a generic query will provide you with plenty of results.

For the sake of a cursory historical review, let's remember some of the beginnings of the WWW search engines. The first one was "Archie" in 1990, leading you to an FTP site, which provided simply an index of downloadable directory listings, but not the contents of each listing. The following year "Veronica" and "Jughead" were added to the short list in 1991, allowing the user to search for file names. By 1993 we saw the advent of "Excite" and the "WWW Wanderer," capable of capturing actual Uniform Resource Locators (URLs), followed by several others added in 1994, including "Infoseek," "Altavista," WebCrawler," Yahoo," and Lycos. Then, by 1998, "Google" and "MSN" joined the list, and in 2009 we saw the arrival of "Bing" in the scene.

A URL is a compact string of characters representing a unique identifier for a web resource (a web server) available via the WWW. The syntax for this string of characters may adopt a variety of forms, such as a sequences of letters, or digits, mixed with special characters.[114] However, the better known syntax uses a series of characters resembling human languages, to facilitate reading and recognition by regular users. In the end, whatever series of characters are entered to identify the URL, the browser will translate the string of characters into the syntax required by the WWW standards.

Modern web search engines include complex algorithms capable of taking an input from your search query and return results that are usually quite accurate. However, let's remember there is another side on this coin; the side belonging to the web site web master, who also has some tools at his disposition. After all, the web master is the boss. But just before we talk about the web master capabilities, let's talk about the entities roaming the global infrastructure of the WWW: the web robots.

Web Robots (a. k. a. Crawlers, or Spiders) are described as

---

114 Bernes-Lee, T, et al, Network Working Group. "Request for Comments: 1738." IETF.org, December 1994. https://www.ietf.org/rfc/rfc1738.txt

cyber programs traversing the WWW autonomously, and web search engines use them to index the WWW contents. This is the good news; the bad news is that spammers and malicious agents can also use the web robots for many other nefarious purposes. But let us return to the previous mention of the web masters. They also use the web robots in conjunction with the web search engines.

Enter The Robots Exclusion Protocol. This is used by web masters in order to provide the web robots with instructions regarding their web sites. These instructions are provided in the */robots.txt* file, located in the top-level directory of the web server. The interaction between web robots and the */robots.txt* file works like this: when a web robot visits a particular web site URL it firsts checks for http://www.example.com/robots.txt, containing instructions for the web robot. Well, at least for the well behaved web robots designed to follow the instructions set by the web master concerning his web site. Of course, web robots can ignore the */robots.txt* file, especially malware robots scanning the web for security vulnerabilities, and email address harvesters used by spammers.[115]

The search engines we regularly use operate withing the context of the WWW, and the WWW is only a subset of the Internet. The proper name is the WWW search engine, because the search is limited only to WWW content, hosted on web servers.

Let us now examine the methodology of a web search engine. A WWW search engine takes a user's keyword and returns a list of web sites that are considered relevant to the search keyword submitted by the user. The acronym for these search engine results pages is SERP. Here's where the business side of the story appears: the goal for many sites is to appear in the first SERP for the most popular keywords related to their business. A site's keyword ranking is very important because the higher a site ranks in the

115 http://www.robotstxt.org/robotstxt.html

SERP, the more people will see it. And you thought that search engines where just expressions of good will?

Enter the SEO, the acronym for search engine optimization. This is the method used to increase the likelihood of obtaining a first page ranking. This is accomplished through a series of techniques such as content optimization, link building, SEO title tags, and others. The purpose is pretty much the same technique than the one used on window dressing on a conventional store; the most prominent items are the ones the store owners wants to entice you to see first, and hopefully, buy them.

Different Internet search engines use different algorithms for determining which web pages are the most relevant for a particular search engine keyword, and which web pages should appear at the top of the SERP. And now, after this cursory review of the techniques used to populate the SERP, and providing the user issuing a query search with a sizeable amount of alternatives regarding the searched topic, what are the web sites getting in return from the user? Yes, here is when we begin exploring the big question: how much of the user's searches are recorded and stored by different WWW search engines? And this is not a new question. Back in 2007 there was an interesting article detailing the policy of five of the major search engines regarding user's privacy.[116]

Some of the spokespersons representing these web search engines stated they would not record the queries entered into their search engine, and added that they didn't engage in behavioral targeting, referring to the practice of offering advertisements based on previous searches used to compile behavioral profiles. Others spokespersons presented a mixed front, stating that after 18 months the user's IP address and corresponding cookie values were purged from their records. Doesn't that make you feel all warm and fuzzy, that after only 18 months your WWW identifiers are

---

116 McCullagh, Declan. "How search engines rate on privacy." CNET.com, August 13, 2007. https://www.cnet.com/news/how-search-engines-rate-on-privacy/

dissociated from the search terms you entered in the web search engines you used? OK, I admit it; there was a little bit of sarcasm in that last sentence. Have we made any progress since then within the last ten years? The answer to this question would rarely receive an objective answer, since there are too many variables, and too many particular interests conditioning the reply.

To protect our search privacy is paramount. A compilation of our searches offers a unique and comprehensive display of our personalities, leading into an invasive glimpse on our private lives. There are options offering a degree of protection to our privacy when using the services of a WWW search engine. For instance, you may configure your browser to reject the placing of cookies in the configuration file of your preferred browser, or to receive a prompt before you decide to accept a cookie from the websites you visit.[117] You may also route all your searches through an anonymizing service. However, the reader must be aware that these options are only mitigating techniques, not absolute solutions.

So, what is the bottom line when using the services of WWW search engines? Remember to maintain a healthy degree of caution, knowing that regardless of your choices and web browser configurations, the content of your searches, and the associated SERP, represent information that is recorded on some of the systems providing you with the search service. You thought the web search engines were developed and maintained just for philanthropic motives? Think again; they are made available as a business opportunity for the entities offering the web search capabilities.

As of September 2016, the Firefox browser offers the choice of private browsing with tracking protection. When a user chooses to browse on a private window, Firebox presents the user with a statement affirming that the Firefox browser does not save data on visited pages, cookies, searches, and

117 USA.gov. "Web Measurement and Customization Opt-Out."
https://www.usa.gov/optout-instructions

temporary files. However, when in the private window, Firefox will save the user's bookmarks and downloads. When In the context of a private browsing session, the Firefox browser presents the user with the following disclaimer: "Private Browsing doesn't make you anonymous on the Internet. Your employer or Internet service provider can still know what page you visit."[118]

So there, now you can see why I previously stated that web masters were enabled to have control on the web sites and pages that were searched. I also stated we would come back to this issue a little later, and now it's the time. So, you thought the WWW search engines were free, right? They are just there, at your beckoning call, waiting for you to enter your search queries, and give you a set of answers, without paying a cent. Well, if you think in terms of using cash or your credit card to pay for this kind of service, then you may be right in considering the WWW search engines as free resources. However, let's not be so naive. Didn't your parents taught you that there is no free lunch in this universe?

The user may not use cash or credit cards to pay for the use of a WWW search engine, but there is another type of currency as important, or even more, than money currency; personal information. As you go your merry way using web search engines to research and locate what interests you, you are leaving behind a wealth of information about you, your preferences, your life style, your personality and idiosyncrasies. How much is that worth, you may ask? A lot, a whole of a lot! On the least threatening side you have advertising tailored to your personal profile created with the information you unwillingly submitted when you conducted your searches. On the more threatening side, you have individuals who may be interested in tracking what you do, what you buy, how you think, etc.

To protect our search privacy is paramount. A compilation of our searches offers a unique and

---

118 Disclaimer displayed by Firefox browser on author's desktop as of 29 September, 2016

comprehensive display of our personalities, leading into an invasive glimpse on our private lives. There are options offering a degree of protection to our privacy when using the services of a WWW search engine.

Remember, there's no free lunch, so someone is paying for all the equipment and the professional technical services of those who make a living maintaining the web search engines working. Since the regular user is not paying, who does? One of the answers is associated with cookies, though not the kind you bake in your oven or buy from the girl scouts. We are taking about the HTTP (web) cookie, or browser cookie.

What is the exact nature of a web cookie? It's a relatively simple data container on a short text-based authentication and identification web site device. A cookie resides on a web server, and it is sent to a requesting client when visiting that particular web site server, and stored in the web browser of the visiting client's cyber device during the browsing session. The main principle behind the concept of a web cookie is for the web server to collect information about the visiting user, and use that information when the same user visits the same web server again. A very simple case of *quid pro quo*; you want something from me? I want something in return.

The web cookie is not a new creation to facilitate web transactions, but rather an adaptation from the world of Unix, where cookies were already in use by Unix programmers. The adaptation into web transactions occurred in 1994, when a Netscape employee adopted the cookie concept to facilitate web-based communication, allowing the web server to identified a client who had previously visited the Netscape web server via a specially tailored text file implanted on the client side, on his web browser, namely, the web cookie.[119]

---

119 According to a Wikipedia article:
https://en.wikipedia.org/wiki/HTTP_cookie

The introduction of the web cookies went fairly unnoticed by the web users, since the newly introduced cookies were accepted by default, and users received no notification of the presence of these tailored text files. It took a couple of years for he general public to learned about the presence of web cookies via media articles, leading to the awakening of the general public via discussions on potential privacy implications of these web cookies, and official hearings during 1996 and 1997.[120]

The privacy concerns rise from the fact that a web cookie may be designed to record details on the user's browsing activity, including particular selections and logging credentials. Web cookies can also record data entered into form fields (names, addresses, passwords, and credit card numbers). This capabilities obviously prompt user's initiatives to question the legal aspects associated with the use of web cookies. These concerns have been deemed serious enough as to generate legal initiatives and legislative actions placed into effect since 2011.[121]

Should the reader desire to research more on the nature and operation of web cookies, there is an official document offering detailed and technical information on this topic. RFC 6265, published in April 2011, constitutes the current and definitive specification for web cookies. This document is a product of the Internet Engineering Task Force (IETF), representing the consensus of this community on the topic. Two specific sections may be of special interest to the reader; section 7, discussing privacy considerations, and section 8, addressing security considerations associated with web cookies. RFC 6265 also makes an important statement: web cookies may appear simple, but they are not void of complexities.[122]

120 Ibid; Hill, Simon. "Are cookies crumbling our privacy? We asked an expert to find out." Digital Trends.com, March 29, 2015. http://www.digitaltrends.com/computing/history-of-cookies-and-effect-on-privacy/
121 Whittaker, Zack. "UK 'cookie law' takes effect: What you need to know." ZDNet.com, May 26, 2012. http://www.zdnet.com/article/uk-cookie-law-takes-effect-what-you-need-to-know/
122 Barth, A. Internet Engineering Task Force (IETF). "Request for Comments:

The privacy concerns rise from the fact that a web cookie may be designed to record details on the user's browsing activity, including particular selections and logging credentials.

Before we close this chapter on web cookies, let's remember there are other cyber devices we use, in addition to our regular desktop and laptop computers; the ubiquitous smartphones, tablets, or any other cyber device equipped with a browser.

There is a very significant difference between your desktop computer and laptop, and your mobile devices, when it comes to web browsing. On the former group the web cookies inhabit your browser environment, exclusively, but on the latter group the web cookies have a more expanded environment, because in addition to interacting with the mobile web browser, they also need to operate in your various apps, and their corresponding environments.

On your computer and laptop, the residing web cookies count on your browser using hypertext markup language (HTML), which provides a uniform environment, and since most residential users use the same browser on the same computer most of the time, a web cookie can interact within a well known environment, within a very stable configuration, and can easily track the user's online activities.

Mobile devices, on the other hand, present a more challenging environment. There are dozens of different types of mobile devices, running different OS, with different mobile web browsers, and each one with its own rules. Additionally, those mobile browsers play in different sandboxes environments than the ones hosting the different apps on the same device, and each of these apps playing in a different sandbox than all the others. Finally, any given user may have multiple mobile devices available, such as a work cell phone, a personal cell phone, a tablet, and possibly

---

6265." April 2011. https://tools.ietf.org/html/rfc6265

a vehicle equipped with Internet connectivity.[123]
The previous reference to sandboxes environments may benefit from a brief description of a digital sandbox. This is a technique designed to protect administrative access to the binary code and data on an app, a very important technique in the environment of mobile applications. The fundamental principle behind sandboxing is to mitigate the exploitation risks associated with the unavoidable coding weakness inherent in any binary code. Thus, sandboxing reduces the attack surface of a binary code by limiting the environment in which the binary code executes. Sandboxing essentially quarantine the activities of a given sandboxed app.[124]

Then we enter another level of complexity, when users' privacy preferences come into play, since the privacy options selected for one app are unlikely to be respected by the other apps, or by the mobile web browser. As of July 2013 mobile devices have overtaken desktop computers for online use, and statistical reports state that from 2011 to 2013, the adult ownership of smartphones increased from 35% to 45%, and the ownership of tablets nearly tripled during the same period. With this trend continually growing, the privacy and security concerns regarding web cookies on mobile devices are likely to increase as well. Do we know how to prepare for monitoring and hopefully managing the associated security and privacy risks?

Until we find a collective and satisfactory answer to this question, the best course of action is to develop and implement a meaningful and effective mindset regarding the precautions to take when using web search engines. Remember the essential principle in using them. It is based on a very simple case of *quid pro quo*; you want something from the web search engine, and the entity sustaining that service? That entity wants something from you, in return for the data provided to you. Therefore, remember that the type of searches, the topic of the searches, and the frequency of

123 http://www.allaboutcookies.org/mobile/
124 Dark Reading. "The Pros And Cons Of Application Sandboxing." 10/2/2012. http://www.darkreading.com/risk/the-pros-and-cons-of-application-sandboxing/d/d-id/1138452?

the searches you conduct become indicators of who you are, and the preferences you have. This type of information may be used to create a profile of your persona.

Chapter 10. The Known Collector

In the preceding chapter we briefly mention the role of ISPs regarding collection of user's data. On this chapter we will specifically focus on the role played by the ISPs in this regard, including the scope and the legal limitations regulating their collecting activities.

Let's begin by conducting a quick inventory of the path your cyber data follows after leaving your cyber system, to send, search, or receive information from the WWW. In order for you to place your cyber data into the Internet infrastructure, and from there search for a path into a web server of your choice, you first have to connect to the Internet infrastructure. However, a regular user does not have a direct connection to this cyber infrastructure. We all need a "middle man" in our geographical area. This middle man takes our cyber data, and places it into the Internet infrastructure on our behalf. This middle man is our local ISP, and the job done by an ISP, in facilitating our connectivity to the Internet sounds great, right? Well, there is a problem though...

The ISP takes our cyber data and places it into its cyber systems in order to establish the connection to the Internet infrastructure. Now, the ISP systems are capable not only of forwarding our cyber data, but also capable of collecting details on the cyber data we place into the hands of our local ISP. In addition to the personal data you provide to your local ISP when you created you Internet account, the ISP can also establish a very complete profile of your web surfing habits, and even the content of your WWW activity, including details on websites visited, for how long, and the contents of the data you view and download. And this is true not only for your residential cyber devices, but your mobile devices as well. So, let me ask this: how do you feel right now about your personal privacy online? Well, take a deep breath, because we do have a little bit of good news regarding a degree of protection for our online privacy.

Section 222 of the Communications Act[125] (amended by the Telecommunications Act)[126] for broadband ISPs contains privacy requirements for the protection of ISPs's customers.[127] On March 31, 2016, FCC adopted a Notice of Proposed Rulemaking (NPRM) to establish privacy guidelines for the implementation of the privacy requirements of the Communications Act. This proposal is designed to ensure broadband customers have strong security protections for their personal information collected by ISPs.

Customer choice is the paramount goal on this NPRM, proposing rules for empowering customers to decide the extent to which ISPs can use and share a customer's proprietary information (PI). To achieve this goal there are two important procedures; the ISP must provide a clearly disclosed and permanent right for the customer to use an opt-out approval regarding customer's PI, and an opt-in approval from the customer before the ISP is allowed to share customer's PI with third parties, or for any purpose outside the ISP's area of service. This arrangement is vital for customers protection, in view of the prevalent practice of ISPs maintaining affiliations with content providers, social networks, or companies serving online ads. In these cases the customer's opt-in approval is required.[128]

This NPRM, comprising 147 pages of text, was adopted on March 31, 2016, with a release date April 1, 2016, a comment date May 27, 2016, and a reply comment date June 27, 2016. The goals of this NPRM are stated as granting consumers the right to protect their privacy, and

---

125 Communications Act of 1934, Pub.L. No. 73–447, 48 Stat. 1064 (1934), codified at U.S.C. § 151 et seq. (the "Communications Act")

126 Telecommunications Act of 1996, Pub. L. No. 104-104, 110 Stat. 56 (1996) (codified throughout 47 U.S.C.)

127 Chernichaw, A, & Apple, J. "FCC Proposes Formal Privacy Regulations for Broadband ISPs." White & Case Technology Newsflash, 19 May 2016. http://www.whitecase.com/publications/article/fcc-proposes-formal-privacy-regulations-broadband-isps

128 FCC 16-39, WC Docket No. 16-106. https://apps.fcc.gov/edocs_public/attachmatch/FCC-16-39A1.pdf

highlighting the responsibility of ISPs for having "access to very sensitive and very personal information that could threaten a consumer's financial security" such as revealing details of medical history, or disclosing this information to prying eyes.[129]

This NPRM proposes rules to give broadband customers the tools to make informed decisions about the use of their online information by their ISPs, and regulate when and how ISPs may share their customers' information with third parties. The NPRM outlines the transparency requirements for ISPs to provide customers with clear, conspicuous and persistent notice about what information they collect, use and share with third parties, and how customers can change their privacy preferences.

In addition to the personal data you provide to your local ISP when you created you Internet account, the ISP can also establish a very complete profile of your web surfing habits, and even the content of your WWW activity, including details on websites visited, for how long, and the contents of the data you view and download. And this is true not only for your residential cyber devices, but your mobile devices as well.

The FCC ruling will simply allow ISP customers to exercise a degree of control regarding internet privacy protections, but does not represent a complete solution to the problem. Let's remember that the ubiquitous cookies remain the main issue when browsing the WWW, as discussed in the previous chapter.

Users must be aware that the online advertising marketplace is dominated primarily by the most powerful web search engines, and by social networking sites. Since the top players in online advertising control 70 percent of the

---

129 Ibid

market, but they do not belong to the category of ISPs, the FCC ruling does not apply to them. If the user chooses to visit these web sites, the collecting problem remains an issue.[130]

This ruling simply mitigate the collection issue only at the first stage of the cyber path, after cyber data leaves the user cyber system and is placed in the ISP systems, representing the gateway into the Internet. The FCC ruling also represents a step forward in joining other countries who took user's privacy protection measures ahead of the US.

On March 31, 2016, FCC adopted a Notice of Proposed Rulemaking (NPRM) to establish privacy guidelines for the implementation of the privacy requirements of the Communications Act. This proposal is designed to ensure broadband customers have strong security protections for their personal information collected by ISPs.

Some of the readers may be thinking at this time that the use of the HTTPS protocol may add a layer of protection for the user's privacy. When a site uses HTTPS, an ISP cannot see the content in unencrypted format, but it can see and monitor requests made to the Domain Name System (DNS). Before examining the DNS issue, let's take a cursory review on HTTPS.

The HTTP is not designed for secure communications. When secure connections are required, HTTP runs over the TLS (Transport Layer Security) protocol, designed to provide channel-oriented security. To initiate a secure communication channel, the HTTP client should also act as the TLS client. Thus, after the HTTP client initiates a connection to the server on the appropriate port, it subsequently sends the

---

130 Learmonth, Michael. "Comcast Rebuke: FCC Rules ISPs Cannot Collect Data For Advertising Without Your Permission." IBTimes, 03/31/16. http://www.ibtimes.com/comcast-rebuke-fcc-rules-isps-cannot-collect-data-advertising-without-your-permission-2346448

TLS ClientHello data to begin the TLS handshake. Upon a successful handshake between the client and the server, the HTTP/TLS connection is established, and when run over a TCP/IP connection, connectivity is established over the default port 443.[131] The TLS protocol is designed to provide communication privacy over the Internet, allowing client/server applications to establish a communication channel specifically designed to prevent eavesdropping, tampering, or message forgery.[132]

Now, let's return to the DNS records issue. Analysis of DNS query information on a per-subscriber basis is not only technically feasible and cost-effective, but actually does take place in the field today.[133] Let's see an example of what an ISP could determine about a person based on domains visited over a short period of time:

Before visiting a web site, the user's cyber device must learn the web site's IP address in order to establish a connection to the web site server. The cyber device client does so by sending a DNS query to the public database that translates domain names into their corresponding IP addresses. This query is recorded in DNS query records, and therefore is available for collection by the ISP of the customer originating the connection request to the web site server of choice. Based on collected DNS records an ISP can very easily create a profile on the user generating the DNS records.

The World Wide Web Consortium (W3C) is the main international standards organization for the World Wide Web. According to the W3C, the standardized text file format for log files on web servers is The Common Log Format, also known as the NCSA Common log format. A simplified sample of these logs files have the following syntax:

---

131 Rescorla, E., Network Working Group. "RFC 2818." IETF.org, May 2000. https://tools.ietf.org/html/rfc2818
132 Dierks, T. & Allen, C, Network Working Group. "RFC 2246." IETF.org, January 1999. https://tools.ietf.org/html/rfc2246
133 Upturn. "What ISPs Can See." March 2016. https://www.teamupturn.com/static/reports/2016/what-isps-can-see/files/Upturn%20-%20What%20ISPs%20Can%20See%20v.1.0.pdf

[Client IP] [client ID] [user ID] [date-time] [client-request]

The section for the standardized time format follows the international standard notation as hh:mm:ss, where hh is the number of complete hours that have passed since midnight according to the astronomical 24-hour format.[134]

For the sake of illustration, let's look at a fictitious and simplified DNS record, arranged in three sections, corresponding to date, time, and domain name:

[2016/09/08 18:44:41] doughnuts.com
[2016/09/08 18:48:22] bagels.com
[2016/09/08 18:48:53] morebagels.com
[2016/09/08 18:50:25] bigbagels.com
[2016/09/08 18:51:27] morebigbagels.com
[2016/09/08 18:55:10] hugebagels.com
[2016/09/08 19:12:12] maps.google.com

This user conducts some very specific web searches to particular types of businesses in the food area. The initial search for doughnuts quickly changes to bagels, escalating into a very specific niche of bagels. So, if the search focuses on large bagels, it is quite possible the user is not concern about carbohydrates, and not a supporter of trendy diets. If the user conducts this systematic search focused on huge bagels, it is quite probable such user is not familiar with the area where the search is conducted, an indicator that such user is new to the search area. A user with knowledge of the area would not have any need to conduct this type of search, since such user is already familiar with the bagel businesses in the area. This conclusion is supported by the fact that he is consulting Google maps to locate the chosen business offering huge bagels.

---

134 This 24-hour system is the world's most commonly used time notation, supported by the international standard ISO 8601, and the majority of European countries. The 24-hour time notation prevents all the ambiguities generated by the artificial adoption of the less popular 12-hour, with its AM and PM time notation. As you may have noticed, in astronomical time, the cycle of the Earth does not stop at noon, to start recounting from hour one all over again, to follow the 12-hour illogical time notation.

Recorded DNS query records are available for collection by the ISP of the customer originating the connection request to the web site server of choice. Based on collected DNS records an ISP can very easily create a profile on the user generating the DNS records.

Now, the time frame for the user's search is also quite revealing. Who wants bagels after 1900 hrs? A look at the calendar shows that the search is being conducted on a Thursday night. So, let us ask ourselves, who wants to locate a bagel place after 1900 hrs. on a Thursday night? Someone who wants to buy fresh bagels early next day, on the way to work on Friday morning, to take them to the working place. At this point we may consider two possibilities. First, since the person conducting the web search is new in the area, he/she is also new in the office place, and he/she is the "new guy/gal" tasked with bringing bagels to the office co-workers on Friday morning. Second, he/she is the new boss, and wants to make a good impression and treat his/her new employees with fresh bagels on Friday.

We could go much further in drawing hypotheses and profiles on this user, especially based on the quick change from doughnuts to bagels, but we will leave that to the imagination of the readers. This is just an illustration on how to build a partial profile on a user's online activity by simply reviewing the DNS records collected by a particular ISP.

Let us now return to the issue of HTTPS and encrypted web site connections. Even when these encrypted connections are established, the corresponding DNS query required to locate the chosen web site are not encrypted. Any residential desktop or laptop is configured by default to use the DNS server provided by the chosen IPS. Therefore, even when this ISP may not be able to look into the content of the encrypted connection, it can monitor the DNS queries the user is generating, as recorded on the ISP's DNS server records. There is a recent paper on this topic, written in generic and non-technical terms, and as such, somehow misleading. When you write about cyber issues, the only accurate language acceptable is the technical language. Generalizations and popular parlance in cyber matters leaves room for misunderstandings and technical inaccuracies. This alluded paper states that the collection and analysis of DNS records are "impractical and cost-prohibited."[135] This assertion lacks technical support. There is a more technically accurate alternative to this non-technical paper.[136]

Current modern networking equipment greatly facilitates the collection and analysis of DNS query records, conducted easily and economically. As a matter of fact, ISPs do deploy a network security DNS monitoring plan in order to detect and protect their network from potential cyber infections.[137] Consequently, and because of the DNS monitoring, the ISP does know what particular web site the user visited online, and that information becomes an indicator required to start building a behavioral profile.

Now, let's consider another possibility, as a means to improve user's privacy protection. How about using a Virtual Private Network (VPN)? The use of a VPN can certainly add another layer of protection to the user's privacy. However, the rate of VPN users in the US is among the lowest in the world, in comparison to other countries. In addition to the increased cost of a reliable VPN, user's should be reminded that even when using a VPN, the site providing the VPN service can also collect information on the subscribers. Thus, we are simply compounding the privacy problem. We have simply added another entity performing collection on our web traffic habits.

135 Swire, Peter, et al. "Online Privacy and ISPs." The Institute for Information Security & Privacy at Geeorgia Tech, February 29, 2016.
http://www.iisp.gatech.edu/sites/default/files/images/online_privacy_and_is ps.pdf
136 Upturn. "What ISPs Can See." March 2016.
https://www.teamupturn.com/static/reports/2016/what-isps-can-see/files/Upturn%20-%20What%20ISPs%20Can%20See%20v.1.0.pdf
137 Ibid

The adoption of a VPN service does not constitute a complete solution to our privacy problem, simply because the efficacy of a VPN service depends entirely on the user's VPN configuration. Realistically, it would be quite difficult for non-expert users to ascertain whether their VPN configuration is properly tunneling their DNS queries and protecting their privacy. This is particularly common for Windows users who, in the majority, remain uninformed on the use of the Command Line Interface (CLI).[138]

When writing about cyber issues, the only accurate language acceptable is the technical language. Generalizations and popular parlance in cyber matters leaves room for misunderstandings and technical inaccuracies.

So, what happens now with our online privacy protection? The FCC web site states that when Congress enacts a law affecting telecommunications, the FCC has the responsibility for developing rules implementing such law. The FCC proceeds to take several actions in developing such rules, by granting consumers the opportunity to submit comments and reply comments to the FCC.

The FCC already released the NPRM, and after reviewing the received comments, the FCC may issue a Further Notice of Proposed Rulemaking (FNPRM), presenting specific issues raised by the comments. This FNPRM opens another cycle for comments on the proposal at hand. After considering the results to both NPRM and FNPRM, the FCC issues a Report and Order (R&O). The R&O may develop new rules, amend existing rules or decline on making new rules. Summaries on the R&O are then published in the Federal Register.[139]

On June 22, 2016 the FCC released a Public Notice announcing an extension to the deadline for reply

---

138 See Giannelli. Cyber Reality. Xlibris, 2016, pp 91-94
139 FCC. "Rulemaking at the FCC." https://www.fcc.gov/general/rulemaking-fcc

comments. The original deadline set for June 27, 2016 is now extended until July 6, 2016. The justification for the extension is to "allow interested parties to respond to the voluminous record in this proceeding."[140]

This extension notice indicates that the NPRM seeking to protect customers's online privacy is becoming a major development in US privacy regulation. Consequently, is generating a high volume reaction among stakeholders and customers as well. This is a strong indicator that this privacy issue is awakening both parties in this important issue that remained dormant for quite some time since the unveiling of the WWW.

A sample of the significant shock wave reaction to the NPRM is the letter from the Internet Commerce Coalition (ICC) to the FCC, dated September 20, 2016. The ICC comprises members from the ISP circle, technology companies, and technology trade associations. These members filed an Ex Parte[141] letter to the FCC, urging this commission to distinguish between sensitive and non-sensitive customer information when considering the establishment of privacy rules applying to ISPs. The ICC letter argues that the definition of consumer PI should cover only certain type of data, but not all data. Furthermore, the ICC also rejects the opt-in obligation for ISPs, since they consider this as impractical and onerous.

When such legal actions are still taking place well after the deadline of July 6, 2016, it appears quite improbable that we will see the issuance of an FCC R&O on this customers online privacy issue. As I write this closing words for this chapter, [142] I consider overly optimistic to expect an FCC resolution by the end of 2016. Perhaps such resolution will be ushered by the arrival of 2017, at a time when the appropriate FCC steps have been completed.

---

140 FCC. "Public Notice WC Docket no. 16-106." June 22, 2016.
   http://transition.fcc.gov/Daily_Releases/Daily_Business/2016/db0622/DA-16-712A1.pdf
141 From Latin, meaning a judicial action initiated on behalf, and for the benefit of, only one party involved on a legal proceeding.
142 October 9, 2016

In addition to the increased cost of a reliable VPN, user's should be reminded that even when using a VPN, the site providing the VPN service can also collect information on the subscribers. Thus, we are simply compounding the privacy problem.

Readers concerned with their protection rights for the privacy of their PI should remain alert to the near future release of the FCC R&O, and upon its release, be prepared to exercise their privacy rights with regard to their ISP. There is a significant amount of energy spent by the ICC members in launching their futile strategy for causing delays to the implementation of this important customer right to privacy. Users should consider employing a similar amount of energy to accommodate the means to restore the privacy rights withheld from users for almost three decades.

Chapter 11. The Wi-Fi Path

Perhaps one of the most ubiquitous forms of Internet traffic is generated and processed through the services provided by the ever present wireless local area network, properly known by the acronym WLAN, and informally called Wi-Fi.

Any iteration of a WLAN environment is based on the Institute of Electrical and Electronics Engineers (IEEE) 802.11 standard, of which there are several iterations, designated by a lower case letter from the alphabet. A WLAN customarily requires an access point (AP) or hotspot, with different ranges, depending on the particular 802.11 standard iteration. These ranges may cover between 65 to 300 feet indoors, and a greater range outdoors. An AP links wireless clients to the traditional wired LAN, thus creating a WLAN.

These ranges can be extended by using multiple overlapping access points. A WLAN may offer data transfer speeds ranging from 1 to 54Mbps on some of the early 802.11 versions, while later ones can offer between 300 and 600Mbps. A WLAN can be configured as a Basic Service Set (BSS), using only a single AP to create a WLAN, or as an Extended Service Set (ESS), using multiple APs to create a roaming area larger than the one offered by a single AP.

WLAN supports various encryption technologies, but some early ones are very weak. Stronger encryptions are currently available (and desirable), with some of them offering an encryption level so high as to requiring dedicated chips to support them. Communication over a traditionally wired network offers security often built into the physical environment itself. A WLAN, on the other hand, cannot offer the same degree of security measures since is operating over radio signals, . As a shared-medium technology, WLAN's bandwidth is limited by the Radio Frequency spectrum.

Public WLANs in coffee shops, hotel rooms and airports face cyber security problems originating in the very fact that they are public, and consequently, opened to everyone. It takes very little hacking skills to surreptitiously monitor and/or hijack communications over a public WLAN. There is a plethora of widely available freeware cyber tools to facilitate the eavesdropping on emails and web browsing. WLAN hotspots present a rich target zone for malicious cyber entities targeting users' data. This condition is usually enhanced and even facilitated by users who routinely expose personal data over these WLAN hotspots.

Consider the following: a user arrives at a public WLAN hotspot, and receives a password login to join the network. Do you think that the password is unique to every user? If everyone joining the same WLAN hotspot is using the same password, then it's no longer a protective password. The arriving hacker will use the same password to join the same WLAN as the other users, and the cyber security of the other legitimate users becomes automatically compromised.

A more insidious cyber attack involves a hacker setting up a public WLAN hotspot under his/her command and control, and made available at the same area in your favorite Wi-Fi watering hole. If the rogue WLAN is setup with a very similar name than the legitimate one, how many unaware users may joint the rogue Wi-Fi hotspot? The consequence to this action is that all those who join the rogue hotspot now have all their emails, site logins, and social media activity being routed through the hacker's network, where the users' data can be monitored and collected. A cautious user would do well in asking a reputable employee of the place offering the hotspot for the full network name before connecting to any hotspot, and carefully check that the legitimate network name matches the one displayed in the Wi-Fi list of available hotspots.

In 2011 a government department hosted a conference on cyber security at a central London hotel. This event, attended by government ministers, senior government security officials, and a range of cyber security experts, among other professionals, obviously attracted the attention of malicious cyber actors. The legitimate attendees came under a cyber attack.[143]

The attack was launched through the free Wi-Fi AP offered by the hotel hosting the event, and executed via the attack vector ARP poisoning, a.k.a Man-in-the-Middle (MITM) attack. This name is quite descriptive, because what actually happens is the attacking system adopts a position of interception between two victim system, by literally placing itself in the middle of the networking path between the two targeted system. The primary objective of this attack is to intercept and control a network communication session. The intended goal of this interception is to access and monitor the network traffic data exchanged between the victim devices.[144]

There is a plethora of widely available freeware cyber tools to facilitate the eavesdropping on emails and web browsing. WLAN hotspots present a rich target zone for malicious cyber entities targeting users' data. This condition is usually enhanced and even facilitated by users who routinely expose personal data over these WLAN hotspots.

The MITM attack can be easily understood when we visualize the process of network connection between two (or more) cyber devices. The network card on the cyber devices have to know the unique identifier of the other connecting device before establishing a network connection. The destination must ultimately be resolved to a hardware address, namely, the media access control (MAC) address of the destination, encoded on each network card. Consequently, ARP broadcast requests are issued through the common networking environment.

---

143 ComputerWeekly.com, The real risk of cyber attack on unsecured networks, Stewart James, November 2011
144 Cisco.com, ARP Poisoning Attack and Mitigation Techniques, Jeff King & Kevin Lauerman

The responsibility for finding the destination's MAC address corresponds to the Address Resolution Protocol (ARP), which allows a host to find the MAC address of a destination node. In order to accomplish this task with efficiency, each node caches a table with the equivalence between the assigned IP address in the common network environment, and the corresponding MAC address of the destination node(s), thus creating a mapping (table) for IP-MAC pair(s) in order to avoid repetitive ARP broadcast requests. However, these cache tables are not static, because there are ARP tools allowing to view and modify ARP table entries on a node.

The MITM attack is achieved when an attacker poisons the ARP cache of two devices, causing each of the victim devices to send all their network traffic packets to the attacker when communicating with each other. This manipulation of the ARP cache actually places the attacker in the middle of the communications path between the two victim devices; hence the name MITM attack. ARP poisoning is a very effective attack affecting both wireless and wired local networks.

The MITM attack in the London hotel was made possible because the affected WLAN, just like many other APs, provided open access without any security controls. This setting pattern is quite common, since the goal of easy accessibility is given a higher priority over secure access. The low cost and availability of wireless routers allows an adversary to set up a free Wi-Fi hotspot, luring users into this hotspot, and launching an MITM. The harvest of all the collected information provides a large number of user names and passwords, which can provide access into corporate networks, and can be sold in the cyber underworld.[145]

If a user wants to ensure that all browsing traffic is encrypted, he/she should consider signing up for a VPN (virtual private network) service. A VPN service acts as a

---

145 ComputerWeekly.com, The real risk of cyber attack on unsecured networks, Stewart James, November 2011

middle man (a beneficial and protective one) between the user and the visited web sites, by routing all communications with an encrypted format. Only after the encrypted communication passes through the VPN server it will reach the desired web site. Someone monitoring traffic over a public Wi-Fi network will see only unintelligible data passing between the user's cyber device and the VPN server protecting that cautious user.[146]

Word of caution: when I categorize a cautious user as the one using VPN service, I do not imply that the simple fact of contracting a VPN service provider constitutes an indicator of wisdom. The use of a VPN server is not a panacea for all issues related to online personal privacy. The issue of using a VPN server is larger and more complex, but a well-thought and well-researched selection of a VPN service provider does constitute an indicator of wisdom. There is a very balanced and well articulated article regarding VPN service that provides sound advice on this topic.[147]

When a rogue WLAN is setup with a very similar name than a legitimate public WLAN hotspot, how many unaware users may joint the rogue Wi-Fi hotspot? The consequence to this action is that all those who join the rogue hotspot now have all their emails, site logins, and social media activity being routed through the hacker's network, where the users' data can be monitored and collected.

A WLAN faces different kinds of attacks. On the one hand we have the case of WLAN sniffers, used to intrude and gather information on the WLAN traffic, while generating no traces of the intrusion. On the other hand, we have the case of a radio frequency (RF) jamming device, designed to disrupt the signal between the AP and the connected nodes.

---

146 NIST Special Publication 800-153, Guidelines for Securing Wireless Local Area Networks (WLANs), M. Souppaya & K. Scarfone, February 2012
147 Krebs, Brian. "Post-FCC Privacy Rules, Should You VPN?" KrebsOnSecurity.com, 30 March 2017. https://krebsonsecurity.com/

A high power RF signal generator will interfere with the AP signal, disrupting the WLAN signal and disconnecting the nodes depending on the affected AP. The MITM attack will place a rogue AP between the legitimate AP and the connected nodes. The attacker will disrupt the legitimate AP, generate a stronger AP signal to lure the nodes into joining the rogue AP, and capture their WLAN traffic.

In summary, WLAN attacks fall into two categories: passive and active. The former is the type of attack in which an unauthorized agent simply monitors the WLAN traffic, without generating, altering or disrupting the WLAN traffic data.[148] The latter is the type of attack in which an unauthorized agent maliciously generates, alters, or disrupts the WLAN traffic. The passive type of attack may possibly act as a prelude for an active attack, since the passive type focuses on gathering information on the WLAN traffic.

The allure and the convenience offered by Wi-Fi hotspots usually overshadows the tremendous dangers harbored in this WLAN environments. The threats are not only present while we share a hotspot on a conventional human gathering such as cafes, libraries, hotels, airports, etc., but they are also present as airborne threats. You may exercise caution while visiting some of these public places, by avoiding to join such "free hotspots," specially in cases when the hotspot is not really visible in the public building, but still discoverable from inside the building? What if your mobile cyber device reports a hotspot from Starbucks, even when you're nowhere near a Starbucks branch? The answer to this question is disclosed in the next paragraphs.

In 2011, while attending Black Hat, this author witnessed the presentation from two security engineers,[149] displaying on stage a functional and tested prototype UAV, capable of eavesdropping on Wi-Fi, phones, and Bluetooth signals. The UAV was equipped with a telemetry link, operating an

---

148 Ibid
149 Presentation by Mike Tassey and Richard Perkins, at Black Hat 2011, Las Vegas

onboard computer running Ubuntu,[150] and configured with wireless sniffers and network-cracking tools.

This UAV is the WASP (Wireless Aerial Surveillance Platform), and it features an IMSI catcher (International Mobile Subscriber Identity) and antenna with the capability to spoof a cellphone base station. Nearby cellphones within range will connect and proceed to route outbound calls through the WASP instead of using the legitimate commercial cell towers. The IMSI catcher is a telephony device designed for secretly listening on wireless phone traffic, and equipped with dual capabilities: it intercepts mobile phone traffic, and allows for the tracking of the movements of mobile phone users. In the case of WASP, it becomes the instrument for airborne MITM attacks, and all for the lower price of $6,000, built in the convenience of a garage!

Does the reader think that this micro UAV might have been just an isolated experiment, grasping the interest of only a few researchers, but never capturing the attention of the general public? Regretfully, this is not the case. We have several current 2015 cases of other micro UAVs that continue the trend of using a rogue AP in the sky. The threat is considerable, to the point of some security companies offering detection equipment to address this new airborne threat.[151]

The low cost and availability of wireless routers allows an adversary to set up a free Wi-Fi hotspot, luring users into this hotspot, and launching an MITM. The harvest of all the collected information provides a large number of user names and passwords, which can

---

150 Ubuntu is one of the many available flavors of the Linux operating system, freely available, offering both community and professional support. https://help.ubuntu.com/lts/installation-guide/s390x/ch01s01.html
151 DefenseSystems.com, New hacking scenario emerges: Wi-Fi signal-sniffing drones, George Leopold, August 15, 2014

provide access into corporate networks, and can be sold in the cyber underworld.

The proliferation of mobiles devices has reached massive proportions, with the corresponding increase in the appetite of users constantly seeking connectivity to APs. This myriad of users provide a very tempting target set for malicious actors seeking to capture their networking credentials and traffic data. The presence of micro UAVs will eventually force security experts to redefine the security perimeter of their residential or enterprise area, to include the airspace above their house or office building.

A security analyst created an interception platform using a quadcopter UAV called "Snoopy." It is capable of tracking Wi-Fi, radio frequency identification (RFID), and Bluetooth signals. It is also equipped with GPS capabilities, thus allowing it to correlate signals to their particular location. The Snoopy micro UAV can eavesdrop on phones, tablets, and a plethora of other wireless devices, such as medical and personal fitness wearables. When operating as a micro UAV, Snoopy can locate and maintain radio contact with the users even when they are moving, or located on a difficult-to-reach location.

An earlier 2012 version of Snoopy, equipped only with Wi-Fi detection, was able to track over 40,000 mobile devices during a single 14-hour experiment in London. New and advanced versions of Snoopy have continued operations in different venues during the last 3 years, including an incursion during Black Hat 2014 in Singapore. This proof-of-concept intercept device is more powerful and cheaper than the earlier WASP; Snoopy comes at a cost of less than $ 2,000.[152]

When Snoopy flies at an altitude of 80 meters is outside the visual range of mobile device users. On a more recent flying operation of Snoopy over London, the intercept device gathered wireless data from approximately 150 mobile

---

152 ArsTechnica.com, Meet Snoopy: The DIY drone that tracks your devices just about anywhere, Dan Goodin, Mar 26, 2014

devices in less than 60 minutes. The collected data included network names, GPS coordinates, and login credentials from Amazon, PayPal and Yahoo accounts.[153]

The best protection against Snoopy and other similar stalking wireless devices is to disable Wi-Fi and Bluetooth capabilities when they are not needed, especially when the user is located in public places. Snoopy is capable of collecting MAC addresses, thus associating the wireless traffic to the specific device with that unique MAC address. Interception platforms of this type can spoof any AP, so cautious users should verify the identity of a public and free AP before connecting to it. If a mobile device announces the availability of an AP with the name Starbucks when the user is nowhere close to a Starbucks location, this is very likely a spoofed AP.[154]

So, the reader at this point may be thinking: it appears I am nowhere safe from wireless interception as I go on my daily life. But what about when I'm traveling by air? We may think that at an average cruising altitude between 30,000 and 40,000 feet we are beyond the reach of micro UAV wireless interceptors. And of course, we are, but are we really immune to wireless interception when we fly at 30,000 feet or more? No, we are still under this type of threat, ever since we demanded for our personal convenience to maintain our network connectivity even when traveling by air. So, since wireless services are available on commercial airliners, we are still exposed to wireless interception when we choose to connect to the airborne AP offered during flight.

Another important aspect of considering this wireless threat is not only the interception of wireless data, but the motivation of the malicious intruder behind the wireless interception. Is this intruder simply looking to collect data for personal profit, or is this intruder acting on behalf of a terrorist organization, or a foreign adversarial government?

---

153 ComputerWorld.com, Flying spy: Snoopy drone helps hackers steal data
    from your phone, Darlene Storm, Mar 26, 2014
154 Ibid

The reader may say at this junction: "Perhaps you are exaggerating the nature and intent of this threat." Am I?

Does the reader knows who owns and operate the system providing the in-flight wireless service? Does the reader knows the manufacturer of the equipment operating the wireless system, or the manufacturer of the network infrastructure sustaining the operations of this system? When we are flying at 30,000 feet, and we are connecting to the AP provided on the plane, to whom are we entrusting our credentials and data?

There is no magic on the in-flight Wi-Fi system. The plane is simply connected to a ground network system providing the connectivity for the WLAN AP located in the plane we are flying. Notice on the following diagram how the entire plane's network system is physically connected, including the avionics and the router providing the connectivity and sustaining the operation of the on-board AP.

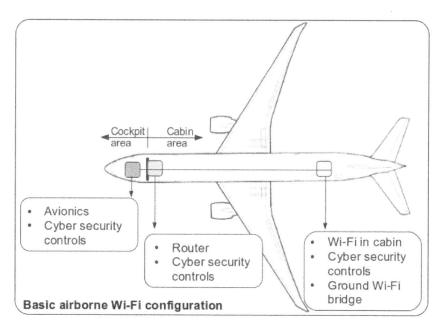

Basic airborne Wi-Fi configuration

So, what are the two most critical cyber security issues to consider? Let us ask:

1. Are the on-board cyber security controls properly

configured to resist an MITM attack?

2. Are the on-the-ground systems and the corresponding operators trustworthy, technically and motivationally?

When considering the first one, do we have any documented evidence indicating that the cyber security controls are strong enough to repel a cyber attack? Let us conduct a perfunctory review on this issue. Even from the early days of the in-flight Wi-FI services there were voices questioning the security of this service, simply because the provider does not furnish encrypted communications between on-board users and the plane's AP.[155]

Is it within the realm of possibilities for a malicious airplane passenger to set up a rogue WLAN AP, in order to implement an MITM cyber attack to gain access to the other passengers W-Fi traffic in the plane? Yes, it is possible. By disconnecting the passengers from the legitimate AP, the malicious actor can force the passengers to reconnect to the rogue AP, and collect their credentials and monitor their data traffic.[156] Someone may argue that in-flight services are protected by firewalls. Is that really an impugnable defense to deter the malicious actor? The answer is no. A firewall is as good as the configuration settings in it, and if the default configuration is the only secure measure applied, then is as insufficient as no security at all.

Is there any other documented security issue that affect not only in-flight Wi-Fi users, but every person on a plane? A reputable cyber security researcher announced the discovery of a backdoor allowing him privileged access to the Satellite Data Unit. This is the most important component of the satellite communications (SATCOM) equipment on an aircraft. This researcher gained access to SATCOM through the in-fligh Wi-Fi network enabled in the plane. SATCOM technologies exhibit numerous vulnerabilities, including weak encryption algorithms and

---

155 Economist.com, In-flight internet: is it secure?, May 6th 2009
156 CenturyLinkBrightIdeas.com, In-Flight WiFi? Not So Safe, Alice LaPlante, June 24, 15

insecure protocols.[157]

Then, when considering the second critical issue, do we have any documented evidence indicating that trustworthiness is not a factor affecting our cyber security protection?

Well, let's start by examining the recent case of the Google engineer flying on Friday, 2 January 2015, when this person connected to the on-board AP and initiated a browser session. She opened a Google search page and noticed a red X over the padlock by the URL bar, indicating this browser session was not protected with HTTPS, the secure protocol for connecting to a web site.[158] Let's remember: this is a Google engineer who knows very well that the Google web site should operate on the HTTP secure protocol. This is a person that understand very well the proper functionality of the Google web site and the HTTPS protocol. And yet, on this session HTTPS was not working properly. Why?

Does the reader knows who owns and operate the system providing the in-flight wireless service? Does the reader knows the manufacturer of the equipment operating the wireless system, or the manufacturer of the network infrastructure sustaining the operations of this system? When we are flying at 30,000 feet, and we are connecting to the AP provided on the plane, to whom are we entrusting our credentials and data?

A successful HTTPS connection to the Google search domain is signed with a digital certificate designed to prove that the data is indeed provided by the Google domain. This certificate provides authentication and protection to provide

157 FoxNews.com, Security expert pulled off flight by FBI after exposing airline tech vulnerabilities, Malia Zimmerman, April 17, 2015

158 TheVerge.com, Gogo in-flight Wi-Fi is spoofing its own customers, Russell Brandom, January 5, 2015; NeoWin.net, Gogo Inflight Internet is intentionally issuing fake SSL certificates, Steven Johns, January 5, 2015

privacy and integrity on the transferred data; this is protection against an MITM attack. The presence of the red X over the padlock by the URL bar indicates that the proper Google certificate was missing. When the Google engineer investigated the root caused of the problem, she discovered that the certificate was signed by Gogo, the in-flight Wi-Fi provider, pretending to be Google. Gogo was actually performing an MITM attack on this on-board customer.[159]

Subsequently, Gogo added insult to injury when confronted by this passenger, and attempted to explain that the interception of the legitimate certificate from Google was in response to their policy disallowing streaming video. This is not only a disgraceful way of redirecting the real issue, but also an insult to the intellect of a cyber engineer who knows very well how HTTPS should work. Gogo is simply circumventing one of the most essential cyber protections, and consequently, voiding their service and operation of all credibility and trustworthiness.

But there is more to the history of in-flight Wi-Fi service. Let's click on the rewind button and go back to 2008, when ZTE, Qualcomm and Aircell announced their collaboration agreement to create the networking infrastructure for Aircell's nascent in-flight Internet service Gogo. Who are these three collaborating entities? ZTE is a global provider of equipment and network solutions, Qualcomm is a major developer of innovative wireless technologies, and Aircell is the leading provider of airborne communications. The Aircell Air-to-Ground (ATG) service relies on a series of ZTE's EV-DO[160] distributed base stations disseminating the networking signals distributed to the on-board Wi-Fi users.[161]

The 2008 media announcement added that ZTE operates these base stations across the US to support service for

---

159 Ibid; TripWire.com, Heads Up Frequent Fliers: Gogo Inflight WiFi Found Issuing Fake SSL Certificates, Maritza Santillan, Jan 6, 2015

160 Evolution-Data Optimized (EV-DO) is a standard for wireless network traffic disseminated through radio signals, and used primarily for broadband Internet access.

161 Qualcomm.com, ZTE, Qualcomm and Aircell Collaborate on Industry-first In-flight Mobile Broadband System, Nov 18, 2008

Aircell's airborne users. The subscriber Wi-Fi network traffic is transmitted to ZTE's CDMA EV-DO networking equipment processed by Qualcomm's aircraft-mounted modems. Back in 2008 ZTE appeared as China's only listed telecom manufacturer.[162]

Well, someone might say: that was then, what about now? Media news from April 2014 announced that Air China flights between Beijing and Chengdu became the first in the country to provide passengers Wi-Fi service during the flight. The wireless connection was provided by ATG network technology. Media reporting stated that Chinese ZTE is the exclusive supplier of the ATG service, through a team agreement with Aircell.[163] So, after after 6 years of their first joint enterprise, ZTE and Aircell are still working together.

The presence of a red X over the padlock by the URL bar indicates that the proper Google certificate was missing. When the Google engineer investigated the root caused of the problem, she discovered that the certificate was signed by Gogo, the in-flight Wi-Fi provider, pretending to be Google. Gogo was actually performing an MITM attack on this on-board customer.

So, what about Wi-Fi now, in 2015? Recent reporting states that Gogo is still providing in-flight Wi-Fi, and extending this service to transatlantic flights between the US and Europe.[164] And according to this recent reporting, the trio ZTE, Qualcomm and Aircell are still working together. This being the case, let us now examine the implications of having a Chinese provider in the midst of this airborne Wi-Fi service.

---

162 FierceWireless.com, ZTE, Qualcomm behind Aircell Gogo service, Lynnette Luna, November 18, 2008

163 ZDNet.com, Chinese airline to offer free inflight Wi-Fi service, Cyrus Lee, April 18, 2014

164 Pcmag.com, Hands On: Delta and GoGo's International In-Flight Wi-Fi, Sascha Segan, March 13, 2015

Why is this a matter for concern? Because the issue at hand is the infiltration of networking technology from an adversarial government that has a long history of antagonism against US interests. The concern has nothing to do with ethnicity, but with the strategic goals of an adversarial regime. The House Permanent Select Committee on Intelligence undertook the official task of researching the foundations of this national security concern, and published their findings on their report, "Investigative Report on the U.S. National Security Issues Posed by Chinese Telecommunications Companies Huawei and ZTE."

This report[165] outlines the threat targeting US national security interests via vulnerabilities in the telecommunications supply chain. The particular focus of the report is directed at the US reliance on interdependent critical infrastructure systems, and the rise in cyber espionage. The report states unequivocally that in this particular context, China has the means, opportunity, and motive to use telecommunications vendors and related products for malicious purposes. The Chinese telecommunications companies Huawei and ZTE are the most prominent exponents of this threat.

This investigative report was prepared and presented by the Select Committee on Intelligence after Huawei published an open letter to the US Government in February 2011. In this letter the Chinese company denies the security concerns raised by the activities, equipment and services marketed by Huawei. ZTE and Huawei are already operating in the US, while remaining under the influence of the Chinese state, or providing Chinese intelligence services access to telecommunication networks. Consequently, the opportunity exists for these two companies to further economic and foreign espionage by a foreign nation-state already known to be a major perpetrator of cyber espionage. The infiltration of

---

165 House of Representatives Permanent Select Committee on Intelligence, Investigative Report on the U.S. National Security Issues Posed by Chinese Telecommunications Companies Huawei and ZTE, A report by Chairman Mike Rogers and Ranking Member C.A. Dutch Ruppersberger of the Permanent Select Committee on Intelligence, 112th Congress October 8, 2012

ZTE and Huawei into the US telecommunications infrastructure is a great security threat.[166]

After ZTE and Huawei representatives where given the opportunity to state their case, through many hours of interviews and repeated requests for providing vindicating documentation, neither ZTE nor Huawei was willing to provide any evidence to dissipate the Committee's concerns.

The persistent penetration of these Chinese companies into the US telecommunications market is a trend that is both suspicious and persistently threatening. Accordingly, the recommendation of the Committee is that Huawei and ZTE equipment, components and services should be excluded from US government systems and from government contractors. Private sector entities, and especially US network providers and systems developers, should seriously evaluate the security risks associated with the products and services offered by either ZTE or Huawei.

Recent reporting states that Gogo is still providing in-flight Wi-Fi, and extending this service to transatlantic flights between the US and Europe.[167] And according to this recent reporting, the trio ZTE, Qualcomm and Aircell are still working together. What are the implications of having a Chinese provider in the midst of this airborne Wi-Fi service?

The multiple critical infrastructure systems sustaining the US population, along with its scientific and industrial basis, are highly dependent on data transmitted via telecommunications systems. As such, they face a great risk by becoming exposed to foreign manipulation on the computerized networks operating their control systems. The aggressive program driving Huawei and ZTE in becoming a hegemony in the telecommunications market, and their ties

---

166 Ibid

167 Pcmag.com, Hands On: Delta and GoGo's International In-Flight Wi-Fi, Sascha Segan, March 13, 2015

to the adversarial Chinese regime, represent a grave threat to US national security.[168]

A major US newspaper echoed the concerns outlined in this government report by stating that, permitting Huawei and ZTE to infiltrate the US telecommunications infrastructure, will pave the road for the Chinese government to easily intercept communications and facilitate cyber attacks on US critical infrastructure.[169]

In September 2012 the US President, based on a recommendation from the federal Committee on Foreign Investment in the United States, blocked the sale of four wind farm projects to Ralls Corporation, owned by Chinese nationals and affiliated with Chinese industry. The Defense Production Act authorizes the president to prohibit acquisitions of American businesses when there is credible evidence that a foreign acquisition might lead to actions threatening national security. The wind farm sites are located in the vicinity of the restricted airspace at a US Navy weapons training facility dedicated to the testing of remotely piloted aircrafts (RPA) and electronic warfare aircrafts.[170]

It doesn't really take much analytical acumen to realize that, behind Chinese-affiliated business initiatives to introduce their products and services into US critical infrastructure and critical locations, there is an obvious and quite transparent intention of infiltrating themselves into the US fabric of life. And since I'm an incurable cynical, I can see a quite evident and disturbing trend in all the activities supporting the Chinese strategy and doctrine of infiltration into the heart of US way of life. There is no need for an external confrontation when you can destroy your adversary from within, right?

So, the next time you fly and use in-flight Wi-Fi service, just remember who is handling your data on the ground stations

---

168 Ibid
169 NYTimes.com, U.S. Panel Cites Risks in Chinese Equipment, M. Schmidt, K. Bradsher and C. Hauser, October 8, 2012
170 NYTimes.com, article by Helene Cooper, September 28, 2012

processing your network connectivity. It's a Chinese company, ZTE, providing the equipment that handles your network data. On the other hand, are you sure you are connecting to the AP provided by the airline you are flying? Remember it is possible you may be connecting to a rogue AP managed by another passenger in the same plane. And based on the experience by the Google engineer, the certificates from the secured site you are attempting to connect may be a spoofed version provided by the in-flight Wi-Fi provider Gogo. Are you sure it is absolutely necessary for you to become exposed to these realistic threats, simply because of the urge for the convenience on in-flight network connectivity?

It doesn't really take much analytical acumen to realize that, behind Chinese-affiliated business initiatives to introduce their products and services into US critical infrastructure and critical locations, there is an obvious and quite transparent intention of infiltrating themselves into the US fabric of life.

The Wi-Fi path is treacherous. Your home WLAN is just about the best chance for a relatively safe trip down this path, provided you are knowledgeable and shrewd enough to configure your wireless router according to the best available cyber security configurations. At least you have a better chance to remain in control of your wireless router. What about connecting to other WLANS outside of your personal control? Well, do you feel capable of navigating the many threats lurking in the waters of the wireless environment? And if you do, just remember who is handling your wireless data...

Chapter 12. The Intercontinental Path

The question before us at this time: is our data traversing the Internet path safer when journeying through intercontinental submarine fiber-optic cables, than when traversing networks across the land? Most Internet traffic, in fact, over 98 per cent of it, is actually routed via submarine fiber optic cables, simply because is less expensive and faster than data transfer via satellite.

Consequently, governments consider submarine cable network as a vital part of critical infrastructure, deserving a high level of protection. As the submarine Internet cables approach shallow coastal waters they become more vulnerable, facing a higher damage risk from a variety of human activities, including ships' anchoring devices, bottom trawl fishing, submarine land slides, and destructive sabotage.

One destructive submarine land slide case occurred on December 2006, when a magnitude 7.0 earthquake caused submarine land slides off southern Taiwan. These slides traveled down into an ocean trench and damaged nine submarine cables, disrupting international communications for several weeks.[171]

The cyber data either generated or received by your cyber system travels an intercontinental path, across the oceans, at speeds greatly surpassing the distribution speed of the first copper telegraph line resting across the Atlantic seabed in 1858. That line allowed for the transmission a few words per minute, but the new transatlantic fiber optic, the Hibernia Express, will allow for 100 Gigabits per second (Gbps) transmission capacity. This is the first transatlantic line built since 2003.

---

171 UNEP UNEP World Conservation Monitoring Centre & International Cable Protection Committee, Submarine cables and the oceans: connecting the world, 2009

So, perhaps it is appropriate to ask at this point: how does the Internet traffic traverses the seas separating the different continents? The answer resides in the deployment of submarine fiber optic cable systems. These fiber lines send signals through a series of pulses of light. The electrical signals generated by cyber systems are encoded and decoded at either end via transmitters and converters. These devices then reverse the process by generating the electrical signals that can be processed by cyber systems at the destination site. The submarine cable system relies on fiber optic repeaters responsible for receiving and re-transmitting light signals about every hundred kilometers in order to avoid distortion and data loss.[172]

There are close to 600,000 miles of submarine cables crossing the ocean floors, forming a submarine path of fast lines, the conveyance of an enormous amount of digital data, facilitating the global interconnection. The amount of digital data is usually measured as bandwidth, and the sum of global traffic has experienced a phenomenal growth rate in the last seven years, going from 11 Terabits per second (Tbps) in 2004 to 185 Tbps in 2014.[173]

As of May 2015 more than 2,000 km of the Hibernia protected cable have been loaded onto three cable-laying ships responsible for placing the new, fast high-capacity fiber optic cable in the designated route, connecting North America to Europe. The delivering of this new service is scheduled for September 2015.[174]

Undersea Internet cables span distances of up to 8,000 miles, and reach lengths of over 13,000 miles, capable of transmitting between 40Gbps and 10Tbps of data across the planet, at latencies of only a few milliseconds. The industry supporting undersea Internet cables are confident in utilizing graphene optical switches to expand the bandwidth total

172 1547Realty.com, How Does Internet Traffic Traverse the Globe? Intercontinental & Suboceanic Connectivity 101, January 21, 2015
173 National Geographic, , June 2015, vol. 227, No. 6
174 BusinessWire.com, Hibernia Networks' Historic High-Capacity Trans-Atlantic Express Cable Deployment Marks a New Milestone, May 11, 2015

capacity to reach into the Petabit per second and Exabit per second range.[175]

Interception of network transmissions on submarine cables is a recurrent event among agencies seeking to collect intelligence on nations perceived as adversarial. During the height of the Cold War, the USSR often transmitted messages between major naval bases directly linked by an undersea cable located in Soviet territorial waters. Courageous US Navy divers from the USS Halibut, a specially equipped submarine, dived 400 feet beneath the frigid waters of the Sea of Okhotsk, to locate and wiretap the five-inch diameter Soviet cable, returning on a regular basis to collect the recorded transmissions. This collecting operation was called Ivy Bells, and lasted from the early 1970s until 1981, when compromised by a former NSA analyst named Ronald Pelton, who sold information on this operation to the KGB for $35,000. Pelton is still serving his life prison term.[176]

Fiber optic lines send signals through a series of pulses of light. The electrical signals generated by cyber systems are encoded and decoded at either end via transmitters and converters. These devices then reverse the process by generating the electrical signals that can be processed by cyber systems at the destination site.

When considering the expenses and risks of using submarine cables for Internet connectivity, the unavoidable question is: why bothering with this expensive and challenging submarine system, when we could use satellites? Wouldn't be easier, faster and less expensive? The development of this two communication systems are contemporaneous 1960s technologies, but satellite communications face the disadvantage of high latency when

175 ExtremeTech.com, The secret world of submarine cables, Sebastian Anthony, September 21, 2011
176 Military.com, Operation Ivy Bells, Matthew Carle

compare with cabled connectivity. The latency for communication signals reaching a satellite orbiting at 22,000 miles in space, and then returning to Earth, is about 250 milliseconds, much longer than the corresponding latency offered by submarine fiber optic technology.

The new Project Express cable is a 4,600 km trans-Atlantic connectivity system built with advanced submarine network technology. It is specifically designed to improve the connectivity performance and reliability requirements of the financial community, offering the lowest 60 milliseconds round trip latency between New York and London. Project Express is marketed as the fastest submarine cable across the Atlantic, reducing the round-trip latency between New York and London to 59.6 milliseconds instead of the current 64.8 milliseconds.[177]

When considering the overall cost of the Project Express estimated at $ 300 millions, someone may ask: is it worth for a gain of only 5 milliseconds faster? For the financial sector firms involved in electronic trading and with exclusive access to the Project Express cable, those 5 milliseconds represent a tremendous advantage, worth millions. When it comes to high level trading firms, using powerful computer systems to search through large volumes of financial data seeking for split-second trading opportunities, then the winning hand is decided in milliseconds. [178]

The Project Express experienced a hiatus due to serious cyber security threats, presented by the inclusion of the Chinese Huawei Marine vendor responsible for the building of the fiber optic cable. Hibernia suspended the work with Huawei Marine in February 2013, after various large US Internet service providers stated they would decline using the Project Express cable built by Huawei Marine. This decision springs out of their concerns on losing contracts with their federal government customers. US lawmakers consider Chinese IT vendors such as Huawei a security

177 Bloomberg.com, Cable Across Atlantic Aims to Save Traders Milliseconds, Matthew Philips, March 29, 2012
178 Ibid

threat to the US, given the capabilities of their equipment to spy on government agencies.[179]

After the hiatus, Hibernia announced in July 2014 the contract with the US vendor TE SubCom to replace Huawei Marine as the new provider for the fiber optic cable. It will provide Internet connectivity and low latency route between New York and London, with landing points at Halifax in Nova Scotia, and Brean in the UK. The new submarine cable will initially provide a transmission capacity of 100 Gbps, capable of upgrading to 53 Tbps.[180]

When it comes to electronic trading, latency determines the winner, because it regulates the time it takes between the starting of a trade transaction and its finalized execution. The lower the latency, the faster the transaction. The quest for a faster means to sort through pricing data is a high priority for high-frequency trading firms. In their pursuit for lower latency, they are willing to pay millions for access to an upgraded fiber optic communications network such as the one offered by Project Express.[181]

The US vendor TE SubCom, chosen to replace the Chinese vendor, has an extensive trans-Atlantic installation experience and a reputable history of successful projects in submarine communication networking. With headquarters in New Jersey, TE SubCom participated in the team responsible for the first transatlantic telephone cable system in 1956. This company also developed and implemented the first transatlantic fiber optic system in 1988.[182]

TE SubCom developed the world's first seamless 10Gbps solution, and it offers the world's only fully integrated cable and repeater factory. In September 2014 the US Navy

---

179 FierceTelecom.com, Hibernia halts cable build with Huawei due to US-China cybersecurity issues, Sean Buckley, February 11, 2013

180 HiberniaNetworks.com, Hibernia Networks and TE SubCom Commence Manufacturing of Hibernia Express Transatlanctic Submarine Cable System, July 21, 2014

181 Bloomberg.com, Cable Across Atlantic Aims to Save Traders Milliseconds, Matthew Philips, March 29, 2012

182 SubCom.com, History, 2015

awarded a contract to TE SubCom for providing fiber optic submarine cable products to support the Navy anti-submarine warfare (ASW) and the US and allied global sonar surveillance, the Integrated Undersea Surveillance System (IUSS). This system represents the first line of defense against potentially hostile submarines, by monitoring sounds in all the world's oceans, with special emphasis on monitoring submarine traffic in strategically important areas. The delivery date for this TE SubCom project was scheduled for July 2015.[183]

For anyone with the will to experience Internet connectivity in the absence of undersea cables, a visit to Antarctica will suffice. This is the only continent without a cable connection to the Internet, and relies on satellite connectivity, offering only a very limited bandwidth and high latency service. A cursory review of average satellite latencies incorporates the three types of satellite orbits, namely, the Low Earth Orbit (LEO), the Medium Earth Orbit (MEO), and the Geostationary Earth Orbit (GEO).

Leo orbit, between 400km to 2000km in altitude, has a latency of 5 to 10 milliseconds. MEO orbit, between 2000km and 36,786km in altitude, has a latency of 30 to 100 milliseconds. GEO orbit, above 36,786 km, has a latency of around 250 milliseconds.

Hibernia suspended the work with Huawei Marine in February 2013, after various large US Internet service providers stated they would decline using the Project Express cable built by Huawei Marine. This decision springs out of their concerns on losing contracts with their federal government customers. US lawmakers consider Chinese IT vendors such as Huawei a security threat to the US, given the capabilities

183 MilitaryAerospace. Com, Navy choosing rugged fiber optic cable from TE SubCom to connect subsea instruments, John Keller, October 6, 2014

# of their equipment to spy on government agencies.

The quest for continuing improvement in fiber optic Internet technology is not a destination, but a journey. And there is an inherent dichotomy to this journey. There are two parallel path; as we find new and better ways to employ this technology, the dark side of our human nature seeks ways to misuse these improvements for malicious and selfish purposes. The collision of these two paths is inevitable, because that's the way we are. However, we do not stop in our search for improvements.

On June 25, 2015, photonics researchers at the University of California, San Diego, announced they have succeeded in finding a way to increased the maximum power on optical signals sent through fiber optic cables, while avoiding the distortion caused by the increase in power attempting to boost the signal. This improvement translates into increasing the distance and the data transmission rates on fiber optic cables serving as the Internet's backbone system.[184]

With the deployment of this upcoming new technology, Internet traffic signals sent through fiber optic cables will travel considerably farther distances without the assistance of the heavy and expensive repeaters used today. In lab experiments, the researchers successfully sent, received, and deciphered information after traversing 12,000 km through fiber optic cables, with standard amplifiers, but no repeaters. By comparison, the newest Hibernia Project Express fiber optic 4,600km submarine cable manufactured by TE SubCom requires over 60 amplifiers. The absence of repeaters also translates into a considerable economic advantage favoring the network infrastructure, leading to less expensive and more efficient transmission rates.

And yet, despite of whatever technical advances we may achieve in improving the fiber optic infrastructure sustaining

---

184 ScienceDaily.com, Faster internet? Electrical engineers break power and distance barriers for fiber optic communication, June 25, 2015

the Internet, there is the ever present danger of either that brutish aspect of vandalism in some cases, and terrorism in other cases. This is the problem of the deliberate physical destruction of fiber optic cables.

As I'm writing this chapter, the media provides us with the information that on the last day of June 2015 we have yet another case of destruction affecting the critical functionality of fiber optic cable terminals.[185] This last case is reported as vandals cutting San Francisco Bay area fiber optic lines, bringing the statistics up to 11 cases in the last year, since July 6, 2014. The importance of these destructive events is highlighted by the involvement of the FBI joining the investigation. Unless the motives and the unveiling of the culprits is clearly establish, we do not know for sure is we are facing vandalism or terrorism.

According to an FBI statement, the fiber optic cables are being intentionally severed, and the culprits appear to have access to the tools required for severing the cables. Vandalism is not customarily characterized by premeditation and possession of specialized tools, is it?

This latest attack, on June 30, 2015, disrupted Internet service for both businesses and residential customers. The culprits gained unauthorized access into an underground vault and cut three fiber optic cables belonging to the ISPs Level 3 and Zayo. On a previous event In April 2009, underground fiber optic cables in California were cut at four sites, disrupting landlines, cell phones and Internet service affecting thousands of customers.[186] Fiber optic lines are protected by robust conduits, requiring specialized tools to sever them,[187] and the affected areas are generally remote locations lacking the monitoring of security cameras. And since the lack of Internet services affects everybody in the targeted area, what is the goal of this wide spread Internet

---

185 CNN.com, Vandals cut San Francisco area fiber optic lines for 11th time in a year, Ed Payne, July 1, 2015

186 HuffingtonPost.com, San Francisco Internet Cable Attacks Investigated By FBI, Reuters, July 1, 2015

187 NakedSecurity.Sophos.com, Mystery vandals are cutting fiber-optic cables in California - how worried should we be?, John Zorabedian, July 2, 2015

outage?

Attacks on fiber optic cable have an impact greater than the obvious Internet outage; the impact could also have a negative effect on the economy of the region and all other interconnected economies, and even reach a level of impacting on the safety of human lives.

According to an FBI statement, the fiber optic cables are being intentionally severed, and the culprits appear to have access to the tools required for severing the cables. Vandalism is not customarily characterized by premeditation and possession of specialized tools, is it?

How many organizations and industries depend on the reliable arrival and dissemination of Internet traffic? Thus, when contemplating this rhetorical questions, we realize that the attribution of these fiber optic cables attacks may go beyond the simple effects of vandalism, and our assessment focusing on simple vandalism may be dangerously shortsighted…

Update to submarine cable status as of March 2017.

Since the time when I originally wrote this chapter there have been some interesting developments regarding new fiber optic submarine cables projects.

Before detailing some of the newest projects we should briefly cover the overall situation regarding submarine cables. There are seven major areas of coverage, defined by any two land masses connected by submarine cables. Each one of these areas of coverage have several submarine cable routes. They are known as the Trans-Atlantic, the Trans-Pacific, the Intra-Asia, the Intra-Europe, the Asia-Europe-Africa, the Asia-Australia, and the Australia-USA.[188]

---

188 Submarine Cable Networks.

One of the relatively recent developments is associated to the perceived impact of the decision adopted by the United Kingdom to withdraw from the European Union. It is known as "Brexit," by merging the first two letters of Britain with the word exit. The Brexit initiative is the result of the referendum held on 23 June, 2016, supporting the determination for the UK to separate from the EU. The mechanism regulating the conditions and timing of the separation is known as Article 50 of the Lisbon Treaty, providing a timeframe of two years for the two sides to agree on the terms of the separation.

Depending on the precise timetable agreed during the negotiations, the UK may achieve the separation by the summer of 2019. Other estimates suggest it could take up to six years for the UK to complete the exit negotiations. This is because the terms of Britain's exit will have to be agreed by 27 national parliaments, a process which could take longer than two years.[189]

UK's Prime Minister Theresa May initiated, at the end of March 2017, the process of separation from the EU, under the terms of Article 50 of the EU's Lisbon Treaty. The official notification letter from PM May was hand-delivered to EU Council President Donald Tusk in Brussels, on Wednesday, March 29, 2017, by Tim Barrow, Britain's permanent representative to the EU.[190]

Though network traffic between USA and Europe has traditionally been routed between New York and London, there are some developments underway designed to bypass the UK. One such submarine cable plan calls for a specific UK avoidance route driven by the uncertainty associated with a negative perception on the impact of Brexit. While there are obviously multiple implications to this separation

http://www.submarinenetworks.com/systems/categories

189 Hunt, A. & Wheeler, B. "Brexit: All you need to know about the UK leaving the EU." BBC News, March 2017. http://www.bbc.com/news/uk-politics-32810887

190 Faulconbridge, G. & Piper, E. "'No turning back': PM May triggers 'historic' Brexit." Reuters.com, March 29, 2017. http://www.reuters.com/article/us-britain-eu-idUSKBN16Z22G

from the EU, some submarine cable designers are seriously considering the alternatives of this separation, and planning new submarine cable routes bypassing the UK altogether.

However, bypassing London is also a strategy not associated with Brexit, but rather with the avoidance of numerous submarine cables intersecting in crowded routes between New York and the UK. The SemanticNet project "Fibre Aylantic" is one such project, offering a direct connection between Virginia Beach and Bordeaux, France, reaching directly the mainland in Europe. This alternate route offers the improvements of new submarine cable routes crossing the Atlantic away from the crowded New York-London route, improving resilience, while offering network services and capacity at a lower cost.[191]

The expectations regarding the final outcome of Brexit has generated certain strategies regarding new submarine cable projects. For instance, a new transatlantic cable has been announced between the US and Europe, with a path designed to avoid the UK, thus seeking to avoid the perceived "chaos around Brexit." Named Brexit-1, this new cable will link New York to Marseille, France, crossing the Strait of Gibraltar.

This new project was announced by an entrepreneur who characterizes Brexit-1 as a submarine cable connecting several cables landing in Marseilles from the Middle East, India and Asia to New York. Brexit-1 promises to have the lowest latency infrastructure deployed between Marseille and New York. The same entrepreneur announced a second new cable project, named Sing-India-Sing, connecting Tuas in Singapore to Mumbai, India. The chairman of the European Subsea Cable Association commented that other future Trans-Atlantic cables are also planning to avoid the UK, given the scarcity of data centers in the UK.[192]

191 Souisa, H. & Etzkorn, H. "The Atlantic: 2017 Infrastructure Analysis." Submarine Telecoms Forum, 2017, Issue 92, Global Outlook. http://subtelforum.com/STF-92.pdf

192 Marquez, João. "'Avoid UK completely, go directly to New York': New Brexit subsea cable to link EU-US." Data-Economy.com, 3 January, 2017. https://data-economy.com/avoid-uk-completely-go-directly-new-york-new-

Other new projects make a similar promise of lower latency, such as the Asia Africa Europe-1 (AAE-1) cable project, announced as being on track to enter service by the first quarter of 2017. The project covers over 19,000 kilometers of submarine cable already laid across the Mediterranean, Red Sea, Indian Ocean and the Gulf of Thailand.[193]

At the end of 2016 there was an article stating a very important observation; quantifying the rate of announcements for new submarine cables constitutes a reliable indicator of the high demand for this type of Internet infrastructure. Even a cursory review of the history of the submarine cables, from the first international one laid across the Atlantic Ocean and linking the US to the UK in 1858, shows us the importance of the telecommunications industry linking countries and continents.

Today, more than a 150 years later, submarine cable networks carry more than 98 percent of the world's telecommunications traffic, providing the essential high-speed fiber optic networks required by both businesses and consumers. These submarine fiber optic cables provide the high-speed service required by our modern society, in addition to the currently feasible degree of security and reliability indispensable to our modern communications requirements.[194]

This demand for additional submarine telecommunications traffic is attracting a group of non-traditional providers, namely, large tech companies joining the ranks of submarine cable providers. For instance, Microsoft and Facebook are financing a 4000-mile undersea cable, the project "Marea," scheduled to run a cable from Virginia Beach, US, to a data

brexit-subsea-cable-link-eu-us/
193 Qiu, Winston. "AAE-1 to enter service by Q1, 2017." SubmarineNetworks.com, 22 October 2016. http://www.submarinenetworks.com/systems/asia-europe-africa/aae-1/aae-1-to-enter-service-by-q1-2017
194 Bayliff, Nigel. "High tide: the state of subsea cables." Aqua Comms, 19 December 2016. http://www.datacenterdynamics.com/content-tracks/core-edge/high-tide-the-state-of-subsea-cables/97491.fullarticle

hub in Bilbao, Spain.

Google initiated this trend in 2010, investing in a transpacific cable named "Unity," between the US and Japan. By December 2016 Google has plans to invest in at least five undersea cables, while Microsoft is planning four, and Facebook two. Amazon recently invested in the Hawaiki Cable connecting Oregon and Hawaii to Australia and New Zealand, according to public announcements. Google and Facebook are joining forces with Pacific Light Data Communication and TE SubCom on the project Pacific Light Cable Network (PLCN). The goal is to lay the first cable directly connecting Los Angeles to Hong Kong. Additionally, Google is also planning on another cable connecting the US and Brazil. The capacity rate for bandwidth is also growing. In 2013 the Internet traffic capacity was at the level of 5 gigabytes per capita. By 2018 this rate is expected to grow to 14 gigabytes per capita.[195]

Improvements in technologies and the increase in the number of submarine cable projects certainly offer an optimistic outlook on increasing bandwidth capacity and decrease in latency, two very desirable parameters for the future growth of the Internet. Besides optimism, we also have to add our efforts in facing the cyber security challenges that will inevitably surface with the increase growth.

Let us then rejoice in the optimistic outlook on an improve Internet experience, with better technologies, greater speed and augmented bandwidth capacity. Let us also maintain a mature, balanced and sober attitude in knowing that all these improvements will also bring new challenges regarding cyber security, and let us get ready to face them and conquer them.

---

195 Ibid

Chapter 13. The Hijacked Path

So, after your data has encountered, and perhaps survived, the many dangers described in the previous chapters, what else could possibly happened to it? It may face the dangers of being hijacked. Cyber data hijacking? Is that really possible? Yes, regretfully so, and it happens more often that we may imagine; it's a sad but concrete fact.

The Internet is a global conglomerate of interconnected networks, literally thousands of them. The Internet is based on a decentralized model, where every connected network is controlled and managed by independent entities. Each one of this independent networks has a unique identity of its own. However, while independent, every independent network requires a connection to other independent networks in order to participate in this mesh of interconnected networks, thus the short name Internet.

Every independent network can provide services to its own internal users, but unless they connect to other networks, they remain as internally isolated networks. Intranet is the term coined to represent an organization's private network, accessible only to authorized members of the organization maintaining that private network. By contrast, the Internet is by its very essence public, consisting of a large number of network resources made available in this public network.

Any independent network requires an internal routing infrastructure and a routing policy, in order to regulate the flow of network data among all its participating members. This routing policy assures the distribution of data within this network, but it also provides a unique identity to that independent network. At the same time, that internal routing infrastructure and routing policy exist in isolation from other independent neighboring networks.

The global Internet is a conglomerate of independent networks known as Autonomous Systems (AS). These ASes are the building blocks of the Internet routing architecture, serving an important role as the critical elements in the distribution of the Internet traffic. RFC 1930 defines an AS as a connected group of a single or multiple IP prefixes administered by one or more network operators, under a single, well-defined routing policy.[196]

The IP prefixes inside an AS corresponds to a set of routers operating under an interior gateway protocol (IGP) in order to determine the optimum manner of routing network data packets within the AS, working in conjunction with an inter-AS routing protocol to determine the best routing flow for network packets traversing from one registered AS to another registered AS in the global interconnected mesh of ASes. The inter-AS routing protocol is the Border Gateway Protocol (BGP).

Within the Internet architecture an AS can also be considered a network domain, and the conglomerate of associated ASes can be considered a collective entity of interconnected domains. The Internet routing architecture, then, can be considered as operating within a dual-level hierarchy; the first level is the one of a domain operating within a particular IGP environment, while the second level operates within an inter-domain environment, regulated by the BGP environment.

The data generated in your cyber system will eventually travel through the routing paths provided by the IGP routing protocol while traversing the particular AS where your ISP resides. Eventually, your data will leave your AS and will travel through the inter-domain routing architecture offered by the Internet, through the BGP collective environment. So, if your ISP resides in AS 2, and the recipient of the data you are sending resides in AS n, then the path your data will follow is decided by the BGP environment. The following graphic offers a very simplistic representation of the inter-domain routing environment. The real global BPG environment is far more complicated than the following graphic representation.

---

196 https://tools.ietf.org/html/rfc1930

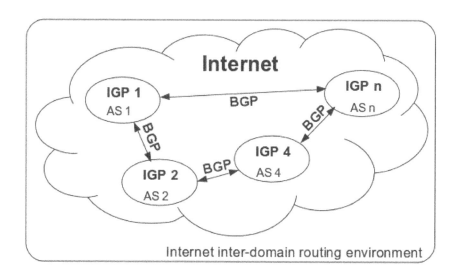

Internet inter-domain routing environment

Each routing domain (AS) represents a single administrative domain, operating independently from other domains (ASes), while at the same time interacting collaboratively with the other ASes. Each of these registered ASes is provided with a unique designator, the Autonomous System Number (ASN). This unique designator identifies every participating registered AS in the inter-domain environment forming the Internet.

The Internet is based on a decentralized model, where every connected network is controlled and managed by independent entities. Each one of this independent networks has a unique identity of its own, and while independent, every one requires a connection to other independent networks in order to participate in this mesh of interconnected networks.

The inter-domain routing environment operates on the basis of two identifiers: address prefix and ASN, corresponding to the IP address prefix assigned to the AS, and the assigned identifier number. The collective inter-domain environment propagates routing advertisements, with each prefix advertising a designated "AS path." Whenever an address

167

prefix advertisement traverses another AS domain, this domain "signs" the prefix advertisement by prepending its own ASN to the AS path. At any given point this "signed" AS path carries the record of a sequence of the connected domains forming the path followed by the traversing network data, from the current point to the originating ASN.

Your data, then, travels from one AS to the next adjacent AS, in a series of steps taking your data one step closer to its final destination. But how does a particular AS determine what is the next step? Using the BGP advertisement system. All participating routers have access to a routing table listing the prefixes accessible in the next step, or hop. The routers along the path announce the prefixes to which they can deliver the packets in the network data traversing the inter-domain path, bringing the data one step closer to its final destination.

A simple analogy for this inter-domain transit process is the concept of a series of mail carriers coming to a US Mail distribution center. Each mail carrier has a particular assigned neighborhood section, so that the most efficient delivery path can be determined for a particular letter or parcel. When a letter arrives at a distribution center, with a particular assigned zip code as its final destination, then the mail carrier whose route includes that same zip code is obviously the best choice for delivering that letter, using the most efficient delivery path. Let's leave this analogy on the shelf for a moment, and we will return to it momentarily.

The network prefixes associated with a particular ASN will obviously be chosen for delivering network traffic identified with a prefix included in the assigned list of delivery prefixes for that particular ASN. Thus, when network traffic arrives at a particular ASN, the advertisement announced by adjacent ASNs will determine the most efficient path for delivery, and eventual arrival at the final prefix destination.

The successive delivery path for any network data packet is recorded by the intervening ASes, using the network address prefix. Thus, the left-most number in the AS path list corresponds to the ASN of the adjacent AS, the one from which the address prefix advertisement was received. The path record will also display a sequence of numbers corresponding to the ASNs propagation sequence. The right-most ASN corresponds to the origin AS that generated the address prefix advertisement. This delivery path record serves a dual purpose: to establish an inter-domain routing length metric, and to generate a loop detection mechanism.[197] The following simplified graphic illustrates this delivery path record.

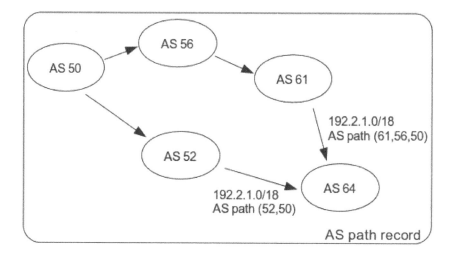

Thus, when the origin AS 50 advertised traffic destined for the prefix 192.2.1.0/18, AS 56 and AS 52 responded by indicating they had a path to that prefix. AS 56, however, had and additional hop at AS 61 before the data packets could be delivered to AS 64, the final destination. AS 52 had a more direct route to the final destination.

Your data travels from one AS to the next adjacent AS, in a series of steps taking your data one step closer to its final destination. But how does a particular AS determine what is the next step? Using the BGP advertisement system.

197 Cisco Systems, The Internet Protocol Journal, Volume 9, Number 1, March 2006

Thus, in the inter-domain architecture of the Internet, routers do exchange route advertisements with each other using the BGP standard, operating between the routers at the boundary between the interacting ISPs. The BGP-speaking routers are constantly exchanging and updating reachability information. Is this orderly, collaborating procedure always this efficient, assuring that networking data packets are transported from one AS to the next and the next until reaching the final intended destination? Of course not! Wake up, this is planet Earth, inhabited by the human race, with a predisposition to transform order into chaos, for the sake of satisfying our selfish and malicious propensity!

Within the Internet architecture an AS can also be considered a network domain, and the conglomerate of associated ASes can be considered a collective entity of interconnected domains. The Internet routing architecture, then, can be considered as operating within a dual-level hierarchy; the first level is the one of a domain operating within a particular IGP environment, while the second level operates within an inter-domain environment, regulated by the BGP environment.

Do you remember the mail carrier analogy we placed temporarily on the shelf on a preceding paragraphs? Well, let's pick it up again, to continue our analogy. Let us say that we have two particular mail carriers, MC1 and MC2, arriving at the distribution center. MC1 lacks the knowledge and the experience of a seasoned mail carrier, while MC2 is a rogue carrier with malicious intentions, planning to hijacking mail from the intended recipients. When the announcement for zip code NNNNN is broadcast, MC1 erroneously take the mail bag and leaves, not realizing that zip code NNNNN is not in his assigned delivery area. When the announcement for zip code YYYYY is broadcast, MC2 takes the mail bag for that zip code and leaves, though he knows very well that such zip code is not in his delivery area.

This analogy will help us to understand the very common phenomenon of BGP hijacking. Sometimes it occurs by accident, due to lack of knowledge and inexperience. However, there are many other occurrences when such BGP hijacking is done with premeditation and malice. What is the end result of BGP hijacking? A massive, illegal misappropriation of network data hijacked by an agent intending to redirect the flow of network traffic data in order to copy it, analyze it, and exploit it.

The core problem associated with BGP hijacking is the honor system regulating the path advertisements. When a BGP -speaker (a border router) announces that his domain includes the particular network prefix advertised as the final destination, there is no reliable manner to ascertain that such router has such prefix included in its assigned routing table. Consequently, the network data is handed to that announcing router for delivery, without any intervening verification process.

Accordingly, it is possible for any AS (or BGP-speaking router) to announce a route for any prefix, and cause redirection of network traffic from other networks sending traffic to a destination included in the prefix advertised by that AS. This is equivalent to the actions of either MC1 or MC2, grabbing bags of mail not destined to their respective delivery routes. The false advertisement issued by the AS in question will cause redirection of network traffic either by mistake or by design, but in either case the result will be data hijacking.

There are some examples of redirection caused by BGP configuration mistakes, such as the case of YouTube traffic redirected to Pakistan on February 2008. Though there was not malicious intent, YouTube traffic became unavailable to most users attempting to reach the YouTube web site: the YouTube data traffic was mistakenly hijacked. But how did this happen?

The problem started when the Pakistani government decided to order national ISPs to block access to YouTube for all users residing in Pakistan. That in itself would not have caused the hijacking of the YouTube traffic, but the implementation of the blocking was done incorrectly, thus causing the unintended traffic hijacking.

So, you may ask, why bothering in devising ways to steal network data from a particular entity, investing time and personnel dedicated to defeat the cyber security measures of that targeted entity, when there is a way to safely and remotely being able to siphoning all the network data flowing from the AS where that targeted victim resides? Well, the answer is: regretfully that methodology is being used more often than you imagine, and quite successfully.

What is the end result of BGP hijacking? A massive, illegal misappropriation of network data hijacked by an agent intending to redirect the flow of network traffic data in order to copy it, analyze it, and exploit it.

BGP routers function on a principle of prioritizing routing decisions. The prioritizing policy states that network traffic is send to the AS with the most specific network prefix. The larger the number in the prefix, the more specific the address prefix. When presented with more than one option, an AS will route the traversing traffic to the more specific prefix.

For example, let us consider two advertised prefixes: 10.0.0.0/16 and 10.0.0.0/24. The prefix designated as /24 identifies an IP address block that is more specific than the IP address block designated as /16. Thus, the advertisement for 10.0.0.0/24 wins over 10.0.0.0/16, and the AS announcing the IP address block /24 will be chosen for delivering the network traffic available for routing.

In the case of the Youtube accidental hijacking, this was exactly the case. Youtube announces 5 different prefixes, namely, /19, /20, /22, and two /24 prefixes. The Youtube prefix 208.65.152.0/22 was the one affected by the erroneous action undertaken by Pakistan. The Pakistani Telecom decided to announced a more specific route, advertising the 208.65.153/0/24 prefix. In BGP nomenclature, a /24 prefix indicates a more specific IP address range than a /22 prefix, so the traffic was sent to the /24 prefix. This Pakistani action created a more specific prefix for the IP address block corresponding to Youtube, resulting in the Pakistani ISP receiving all the Youtube traffic, a network traffic redirection cause by the configuration mistake.[198]

The network data interception and hijacking offers the perpetrators the opportunity for weaponizing the accidental Pakistani-Youtube hijacking, intercept a victim's traffic, invest a little time to inspect, copy or modify it, and then resend the intercepted data to the intended recipient. During 2013 there were more than 1,500 individual IP address blocks compromised by hijacking activity, by perpetrators operating from various countries, during events lasting from a few minutes to several days. There have been over 150 cities with at least one victim of a confirmed Man-in-the-Middle (MITM) route hijacking attack. The target set includes financial institutions, Voice over IP (VoIP) providers, and world governments.[199]

When it comes to BGP hijacking, even fiber optic tapping becomes unnecessary. Why bother in acquiring specialized equipment and personnel to execute a submarine fiber optic tapping operation, when it's possible for the hijacker to execute commands from a BGP-speaking router? The victim(s) should not even notice the increase in latency resulting from the network data interception. It's possible to redirect Internet traffic halfway around the world, copy it, inspect it, modify it, and then resend it to its intended final destination. There are several recent cases to confirm this type of illegal hijacking. After all, how many enterprises are

---

198 DynResearch.com, Pakistan hijacks YouTube, Martin Brown, February 24, 2008
199 DynResearch.com, The New Threat: Targeted Internet Traffic Misdirection, Jim Cowie, November 19, 2013

monitoring the expected latency and the routing path their network traffic should take when traversing the Internet?

Let's begin with the Belarus case. In February 2013, an observable sequence of events took place, with a duration encompassing from just a few minutes to several hours. The recorded evidence shows that global traffic was redirected to the Belarusian ISP GlobalOneBel. These redirection events maintained an almost daily schedule, throughout the entire month. The target set of the hijacking entity included major financial institutions, network service providers, and governments from an array of countries. Among the list of targets were the US, Germany, South Korea, the Czech Republic, Libya, Iran, and Lithuania.[200]

Let's look at the case of hijacking traffic between Mexico and Washington DC, but redirected to Moscow. The normal routing path calls for the Mexican ISP Alestra to pass the traffic to PCCW in Texas, and from there routed to Washington, DC, where Qwest/Centurylink makes the final delivery to the recipient. Instead, the network traffic took a much longer route.

The ISP in Texas handed the traffic to Level3, but this AS is announcing a false Belarus route, advertised by Russia's TransTelecom, in response to an advertisement from their customer, Belarus Telecom. Based on the advertised routing, Level3 passed the traffic to London, and from there it was delivered to Transtelecom. This AS then proceeds to send the hijacked traffic to Moscow and then on to Belarus. The Belarusian AS Beltelecom examines the data in the hijacked traffic, and then returns it through a "clean path" via the Russian provider ReTN. On the return path, this Russian ISP delivers the hijacked traffic to Frankfurt and hands it to NTT for delivery to New York. NTT passes the traffic to Qwest/Centurylink in Washington DC, for its final delivery.

---

200 Ibid

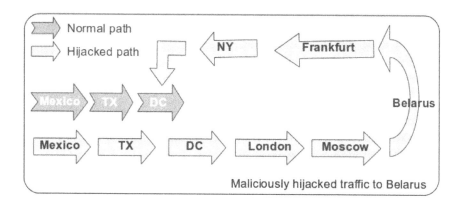

Maliciously hijacked traffic to Belarus

This event is properly recorded, and the evidence is openly available, to prove this is not a case of a configuration mistake, but rather a premeditated hijacking of network traffic, taken literally around the world, involving a circuitous routing path, designed to hijack data through illegal means.[201] Of course, the very moment I raise this argument of illegal means there will be a throng of attorneys claiming that without legislation in BGP routing I cannot raise the argument of illegality. Well, that being the case, let us settle this argument by categorizing this hijacking action as malicious, deceptive, and unauthorized. Is everybody happy now? But on the other hand, do attorneys understand BGP routing?

The traffic hijacking from Belarus continued until March, with some brief recurrences in May, only to be replaced by other brief BGP hijacking event originating from an Icelandic ISP. Then, at the end of July 2013, another small Icelandic ISP began advertising routes for almost 600 IP networks. This malicious advertising is quite evident by the fact that this small Icelandic ISP handles on any normal day only 3 IP networks. The Icelandic ISP was maliciously advertising 600 IP networks owned by one of the largest VoIP provider in the US. There were 17 BGP hijacking events from Iceland, covering from July 31 to August 19, 2013.

There were nine different Icelandic ASes involved in these premeditated BGP hijackings, affecting victims in several

---

201 DynResearch.com, The New Threat: Targeted Internet Traffic Misdirection. This article contains a traceroute record that is incontrovertible.

different countries, and following the same methodology of announcing false routing paths, leaving 'clean paths' to North America in order to return the redirected network traffic to the original intended recipients.

It's possible to redirect Internet traffic halfway around the world, copy it, inspect it, modify it, and then resend it to its intended final destination. There are several recent cases to confirm this type of illegal hijacking. After all, how many enterprises are monitoring the expected latency and the routing path their network traffic should take when traversing the Internet?

There is even a more shocking and blatant case of BGP hijacking, bordering into the ludicrous. This event involves two entities in Denver, CO, located across town from each other, and exchanging network data. And yet, after the originator placed the data into the routing path, the network traffic intended to simply go across town, it is hijacked to Iceland, before eventually returning to Denver after a long detour path. How is that possible?

The Icelandic ISPs hijacked a block of IP address space belonging to Qwest/Centurylink in Denver. The other Denver ISP Atrato received a false route path to the hijacked IP address block from the malicious Icelandic ISP. When the Atrato customer sends network traffic across town to the recipient party, the Atrato ISP sends the traffic to London instead, misguided by the false route advertisement received from the Icelandic ISP. From the ISP in London the hijacked traffic is passed to the malicious Icelandic ISP that originated the false route advertisement.

After the traffic in Iceland is processed according to the nefarious agenda of the Icelandic culprit, the hijacked traffic is returned to Montreal on a "clean path" to Cogent via the Greenland Cable. In Montreal Cogent receives the hijacked traffic and sends it to Chicago. From there it is routed to

New York, and received by Qwest/Centurytel. Finally, Centurytel delivers the hijacked traffic across the USA through Dallas and Kansas City, to arrived at the intended recipient in Denver, just across town from the originator.

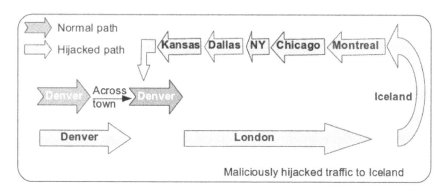

Maliciously hijacked traffic to Iceland

Based on the collected evidence and the traceroute record, covering both the Belarusian and the Icelandic hijackings, there is absolute certainty about the malicious intent of these network traffic redirections. These 21 Belarusian events (February and May 2013), and 17 Icelandic events (July and August 2013) did not happened by accident; they were premeditated and persistent BGP hijacking attacks.[202]

These BGP route hijacking events take place on a regular basis, but they are not always detected and recorded. Thus, we are left with a concrete threat at a global level, affecting both individuals and organizations. Furthermore, this is not just a threat to the intended route of network traffic, but primarily to the data transported by the network traffic. Any organization with sensitive proprietary data is at risk, and banks or credit card processing companies are equally exposed to this threat. Additionally, any government agency is facing the same threat posed by BGP hijacking. Are any of these affected entities maintaining a proactive monitoring of the global routing of their advertised IP prefixes? Do they have the professionally and technically qualified personnel to conduct this type of monitoring?

The BGP hijacking attack leaves permanent and recordable footprints in the global routing environment, pointing right

---

202 Ibid

back to the origin of the interception. However, the culprits engaged in conducting these interceptions do so because they know the footprint of their actions are not under scrutiny. Are they correct in holding this assumption?

BGP hijacking can easily be categorized as the biggest security threat in Internet communications. This threat is stealthy, can reach a global scale, can go undetected, and allow the surreptitious monitoring of unencrypted Internet traffic anywhere in the world, allowing the perpetrators to even modify the hijacked traffic data before arriving at its intended destination.[203]

The BGP hijacking method can be applied to a number of different agendas, including corporate and even nation-state espionage, orchestrated by intelligence agencies looking to collect Internet data without the cooperation of ISPs. How many ISPs are actually and proactively monitoring their BGP exchange routes?

Two network security experts demonstrated a BGP hijacking session during the 2008 DEFCON event in Las Vegas. They intercepted the network traffic sent to the DEFCON network and redirected it to a system under the control of these two researchers in New York, and then they rerouted the hijacked network traffic back again to DEFCON in Las Vegas.[204]

BGP route hijacking events take place on a regular basis, but they are not always detected and recorded. Thus, we are left with a concrete threat at a global level, affecting both individuals and organizations. Furthermore, this is not just a threat to the intended route of network traffic, but primarily to the data transported by the network traffic. Any organization with sensitive proprietary data is at

203 Zetter, Kim. "Revealed: The Internet's Biggest Security Hole." Wired.com. August 26, 2008. https://www.wired.com/2008/08/revealed-the-in/
204 Ibid

risk, and banks or credit card processing companies are equally exposed to this threat. Additionally, any government agency is facing the same threat posed by BGP hijacking.

It may come as a surprise to some readers, but when conducting a BGP hijacking there is no vulnerability exploitation involved. This technique simply exploits the natural design of the BGP methodology, based primarily on trust. BGP operates on the assumption that when a BGP-speaking router advertises the best and quickest (the more specific) path between origin and destination, that router actually has the officially assigned best path. BGP cannot discern when a BGP-speaking router advertises a deceptive message.

Perhaps the worst part is that warnings about this cyber security threats do not resonate with either the population in general, or leadership in particular. For instance, Peiter "Mudge" Zatko, a computer security expert testified before Congress in 1998 that he could cause serious disruption to the Internet in 30 minutes using a BGP attack. He also disclosed privately to government agents how BGP could also be exploited to eavesdrop, and described the details of this type of attack to intelligence agencies and to the National Security Council.

Stephen Kent, an information security scientist at BBN Technologies, conducted a private demonstration of a similar BGP interception for the Departments of Defense and Homeland Security a few years ago. So, those who know how to detect and prevent these BGP hijacking events are creating situational awareness among our government leadership. And yet, case after case of BGP hijacking continues to happen. What is the reason for this apathy? We don't care? We don't understand the serious implications of this threat? We don't respond to the criticality of this serious threat to our national interests?

When conducting a BGP hijacking there is no vulnerability exploitation involved. This technique simply exploits the natural design of the BGP methodology, based primarily on trust. BGP operates on the assumption that when a BGP-speaking router advertises the best and quickest (the more specific) path between origin and destination, that router actually has the officially assigned best path. BGP cannot discern when a BGP-speaking router advertises a deceptive message.

Remember, when we created the foundational technologies enabling the Internet functionality, we were living in a state of innocence. We were simply delighted in the perspective of establishing a global means of communication, and malice and selfishness were not on the design board. However, these negative aspects of our human nature began to surface, and now they freely roam the cyber network landscape. The BGP architecture is built on a principle of trust, but that trust is being exploited by malicious agents.

Though it is not my intent to initiate a polemic on the controversial attribution[205] on the following popular quote, it is fitting to close this chapter by reiterating it:

The only thing necessary for the triumph of evil is for good men to do nothing.

2017 BGP hijacking threat mitigation update

On September 2017 the IETF published RFC 8206, addressing the methodology for the implementation of a secure paradigm to ensure the AS migration into a more secure environment within the BGPsec protocol, RFC 8205.

---

205 Popularly attributed to the 18th century Irish philosopher Edmund Burke, though not unanimously accepted.

The purpose of implementing this protocol is to offer protection against modifications into the BGP AS_PATH, "whether by choice, by misconfiguration, or by malicious intent."[206]

The IETF offers this migrating solution by implementing a BGPsec path validation strategy requiring each router in the AS path to cryptographically sign any update, thus asserting that every AS on the path of ASes "listed in the UPDATE message has explicitly authorized the advertisement of the route to the subsequent AS in the path."[207]

Will ISPs, both regionally and globally, embrace and adopt this BGPSec path validation strategy? The mitigation for the BGP hijacking is now designed. Will it be implemented?

---

206 https://tools.ietf.org/pdf/rfc8206.pdf
207 Ibid

Chapter 14. Data Remanence

Yes, we have come to the point where we complete a full circle, after having generated or received data that traversed the global Internet, and was processed by a myriad of cyber devices. And now, after a certain time of using our cyber device(s), we come to the realization that these devices have reached the end of their life cycle; consequently, we have decided it's time to upgrade to a new cyber system!

We may consider that since our current cyber system is no longer adequate for our use, it is still a working cyber device that may be useful to other users, and we decide to either sell or donate our device. However, one important consideration requires our attention; the purging of the data stored in the cyber system we are now planning to make available to other users.

That sored data is certainly important to us, and so we make back up copies of it. But after backing up the data, what do we do with the original data still stored in the system's storage device we are about to decommissioned? The clear answer is: we need to sanitize the storage device before we place the cyber system in the hands or someone else. Some reader may volunteer a comment and say: let's delete the data before we deliver our system into someone else's hand. Simple, right?

No, it's not that simple. The right answer will depend on the type of storage device used on the system you are decommissioning. At the present time there are primarily two types of storage devices on cyber systems: the traditional Hard Disk Drive (HDD) and the newer Solid State Drive (SSD). The main concern during the data sanitization process is to mitigate the risk of data remanence. The most dangerous myth among uninformed users is to assume that once we issue a delete command in our cyber systems the target data is permanently destroyed. That is not the case. After a deletion command, the data remains in the storage device, and can be recovered and extracted.

The shocked reader may say: But how is that possible? I thought that delete means delete! Not really. That is only an expression, not an actual description, to indicate that the OS has marked the target data for deletion at a future date, after certain conditions are met, and those certain conditions are different depending on whether you have a traditional HDD or a newer SSD storage device. The window for the data remanence risk is the time frame between the moment when the OS marks the selected data for deletion, and the time when the actual deletion occurs. Between these two separate events the discarded data is still discoverable and recoverable.

This risk is the result of the design implemented in several OS and file managers, seeking to assist the user of a cyber system with the capability to reverse data loss in the event of an unintended erasure. This design facilitates a recovery methodology by moving data selected for deletion to a holding area from where the legitimate user can recover this so-called "deleted" data.

So, let's just start with the cliché statement: I have bad and good news. Which one do you want first?

The good news is that you purchase a cyber system under the premise that you will have full control on it, or at least that's the impression most cyber systems users have. The bad news is that you may certainly own the hardware comprising your personal cyber system, and you also may have some degree of control on the data you generate in that cyber system, but full control on the data stored in that system ... Well, that's a completely different story.

Control of the data generated on that cyber system you own is not entirely a prerogative of the system's owner. Let's examine some foundational details on the principles of data storage on a cyber system. One of the main principles to keep in mind is the distinction between magnetic and logical data storage, as the two methodologies corresponding to the two types of storages known as HDDs and SSDs, respectively.

Now, let's remember we are dealing with the issue of data remanence, that is, the data set that may remain in the storage device we have decided to decommission, and we need to plan the best available procedure to destroy such data set, in order to allow another user to acquire the system we are decommissioning. The destruction of the data set, the data sanitization process, must provide the original owner with the absolute guarantee that the storage device contains no discoverable and recoverable information.

The process of data sanitization is quite different on either an HDD or a SSD storage device. The good news for those who are still using a traditional HDD is that there are multiple choices for data sanitization, supported by a significant number of effective sanitization methodologies. However, the risks of malfunction on a traditional HDD are higher than on a SSD; the former is a very complicated systems, with multiple moving mechanical parts, exposed to wear and tear, vibrations, shock, and other failure risks. The latter, without moving parts, is more efficient, more stable, and exposed to fewer failure risks that an HHD.

Well, a user may think, if that's the case, then the SSD is definitely the winner. Such an opinion is definitely accurate is the user knows how to perform an effective data sanitization process on a SSD storage device. If, on the contrary, the user does not possess such knowledge, that's when the story start getting complicated.

Why, you may ask? Because the terminology we use to describe our attempts to perform data sanitization (data destruction) on a cyber storage device generates a misconception, misleading us into a false sense of security. This is the bottom line: data we store on an HDD cannot be truly removed. Instead, the OS renders the data selected for deletion inaccessible to the user via the OS, thus creating only the impression that the selected data is erased. This is the real problem behind the issue of data remanence; the data that remains in the storage device, but is rendered inaccessible to the user.

Every user of a cyber storage device must gain the proper understanding of the data remanence issue in order to take the appropriate and effective measure to ensure that data in a storage device remains inaccessible to unethical hands attempting to collect it. The data residing on any cyber storage device should be available only to the legitimate owner of such data.

The presence of data remanence on a HDD in a cyber system represents a potential security risk for any person or business. But since safe procedures for data sanitization on HDDs are abundant, we will concentrate on discussing data sanitization on SSDs. Why? Because with the advent of SSDs, a new chapter in data remanence is open. The traditional ways of purging data from HHDs is no longer applicable to SSDs.

… you may certainly own the hardware comprising your personal cyber system, and you also may have some degree of control on the data you generate in that cyber system, but full control on the data stored in that system … Well, that's a completely different story.

When a user in 2016 feels inclined to search for official government standards on guidance regarding data sanitization, the search will prove difficult, as all such published standards were written several years ago, some of them as early as the 1990s, and the relatively most recent ones were written in 2006 and 2008. For this reason any information regarding SSD sanitization is absent in such standards. This is because the evolutionary path of SSD technology, from its early stages, was available only to high-end environments, and later, into the current NAND-based architecture, available to consumers in general, would not appeared until 2008.

With the growing adoption of SSDs in cyber systems ranging from desktop computers to cloud storage, data remanence on SSDs becomes even more crucial to the security concerns of both individuals and businesses. Incorrectly applying HDD data sanitization techniques to a SSD storage device will only render the data more vulnerable, by increasing either personal or enterprise risks, and by generating a false sense of security.

Data is recorded magnetically on a HDD, and since the magnetic field of the platters of the HDD can be altered, we can then facilitate the operations we familiarly call writing, overwriting and deleting of data. With the advent of the SSD technology, a whole new procedure comes into play. The SSD technology does not rely on magnetic fields. Instead, it uses flash memory by electrically storing bits of data in many arrays of memory cells. This is why there are no moving parts on a SSD storage device, because it does not require mechanically moving pieces to accomplish the operations of writing, altering, and accessing data. On a SSD storage device, the data is accessed directly from the memory cells, thus providing a faster access speed rate than on a HDD.[208]

This storage methodology difference requires a completely different approach when dealing with the issue of data remanence and sanitization for data residing in either a HDD or a SSD. Data sanitization on a HDD requires the overwriting of stored data with new data, but this overwriting process is unfeasible in a SSD, simply because flash memory cannot be overwritten. Why, you may ask? Because in a SDD storage device data changes are written to a different location on the SDD, not overwritten on the same location. After processing the data change, the flash translation layer updates the mapping for the location of the new data, thus rendering the changed data inaccessible to the cyber system, even though this older data still resides on the host system.

208 Seaber, Garry. "Ghosts of Data Past, pt. 2 – Data Remanence on SSDs."
     March 7, 2014. http://www.itliquidators.com/blog/data-remanence-on-ssds/

Simplified diagram of a SSD Storage Device

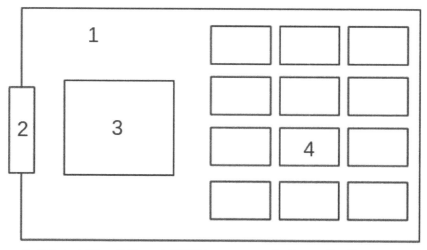

1. Printed Circuit Board (PCB)
2. Interface with cyber host system
3. Controller/Processor
4. NAND Memory Cells

So, you may ask, if you own a system with SSD technology, how do you effectively sanitize data in your system, and protect your personal privacy, by avoiding retrieval of data by unauthorized individuals? The answer is not simple, and the process is not easy.

The uniqueness of SSD technology faces the owner of the cyber system with a unique set of challenges requiring a specialized set of data destruction techniques. The advantages of SSD technology demands a heavy price when it comes to data sanitization. Perhaps this is the best time to introduce one of the most important components in SSD technology; the Flash Translation Layer (FTL).

Another translator? We are dealing with a new SSD storage technology, so why do we need a translator? The answer is quite simple. We do have a new cyber storage technology, but the host system still operates with traditional OS and file systems designed to operate and interact with traditional HDDs, which arrange data storage in sectors. So, what is the problem? SSD does not arrange data storage in sectors!

The arrival of SSD technology did not happen in a vacuum; it arrived in the context of traditional OS and file systems, both designed to operate within the environment of a hard drive with data located on specific sectors. So, how would a traditional OS and file system find data located on a storage media that is not a disk and does not arrange data in sectors? Enters FTL, the emulator, translator and middle man allowing a traditional OS and file system to "see" the SSD as if it was a traditional disk storage media, even though it isn't.

SSD stores data in a unit called a "page," and each page is arranged in a group of pages forming a "block." On SSD technology, data is written in pages, but it can only be erased in blocks. The FTL then coordinates the communication between the NAND memory cells and the host system, by implementing the dynamic mapping system between the Logical Block Addressing (LBA) and the Physical Block Address (PBA).

A host cyber system expects to access data on an HDD configured in sectors, while the SSD storage device actually is arranged in blocks and pages. Thus the importance of the FTL on a SSD, as the agent responsible for translating a sector access command from a traditional OS/file system into the newer page or block access command required by SSD architecture.

Since we are actually writing to a page and not a sector, we must create a map of the address corresponding to the location where the host "thinks" has written data, based on the host traditional sector-based architecture. The truth is that the SSD controller has written the data to an address corresponding to a NAND memory cell location. The FTL is responsible for keeping metadata mapping the exact location of the written data.

This task is what makes the FTL such an important agent, as the high performance NAND flash data manager, allowing traditional OS and sector-based file systems (FAT, NTFS, etc.) to interact with the new NAND flash memory environment, providing the necessary emulation to make it appear to the host OS and file system as if it was a sector-based drive environment.

Since the Flash Translation Layer (FTL) on a SSD controls how the cyber system can access the stored data, this layer exercises the prerogative of effectively "hiding" data from software data destruction techniques. For this reason, SSD manufacturers include built-in sanitization commands designed to sanitize data on the SSD, by enabling a path that avoids the interference presented by the flash translation layer.[209]

So, you start sensing a glimmer of hope, right? Well, sorry to burst your bubble, but those SSD built-in sanitization commands work pretty well in theory, but in practice …? That's a different story. If these commands are improperly designed, or if they are improperly implemented, the erasure techniques will not be effective, and you may be left with the impression that the sanitization process was executed successfully, when indeed the data selected for erasure is still residing in the flash memory cells. This is why the issue of data remanence remains a serious challenge when stored in SSDs. However, do not lose hope. There is a very simple solution, but is neither pleasant, nor elegant. Yet, it is a 100% effective. I will tell you about it a little bit later...

For the moment, let's try to understand the general structure in a cyber storage device. Before engaging in the topic of data sanitization on a modern cyber storage device, be it an HDD, a SSD or a flash-based USB stick, we have to understand the layers comprising the internal organization on the cyber storage device. On an HDD, the hardware layer is where blocks are normally defined during the manufacturing process, becoming hard divisions set by the factory, and programmed into the storage device's controller. In the case of a SSD storage device, a block is comprised of a number of pages, represented by a number of individual NAND cells.[210]

---

209 Ibid

210 Hutchinson, Lee. Ask Ars: "My SSD does garbage collection, so I don't need TRIM… right?" Ars Technica, 4/27/2015.
http://arstechnica.com/gadgets/2015/04/ask-ars-my-ssd-does-garbage-collection-so-i-dont-need-trim-right/

So, let's talk a little bit about NAND cells. NAND flash memory is a type of non-volatile memory, capable of maintaining stored data in the absence of electric power. This technology is also present in smartphones and USB thumb drives. This non-volatility capability is possible by using floating gate transistors, which create a tiny cage (the floating gate), and encouraging electrons to migrate into or out of that cage, using a particular quantum tunneling effect. The charge represented on those electrons remains permanently trapped inside the cage, even in the absence of electric power. Each transistor stores a single bit, a "1" (uncharged cell), or a "0" (charged cell). Data storage is therefore achieved by combining a large number of them. Since NAND flash is designed to read and write data only one page at a time, NAND chips can only accept commands structured to regard pages as the smallest addressable unit. A page of NAND flash is physically made up of a row of cells.[211]

When it comes to NAND cells, we have to understand the layers of control required to access data on a modern SSD storage device. These layers can be simplistically defined as three concentric rings, with the inner circle having direct full control and accessibility to all the store data, the middle ring having only a logical limited access granted by the inner circle, and the outer circle offering a very indirect limited access, with very limited visibility into the stored data. Guess what: you, the legitimate owner of the cyber system and its storage device, are seating on the outer circle, so you have only very indirect limited access!

A SSD storage device can read and write at the page level, but cannot erase at the page level. The SSD technology limits the data erasing procedure to be implemented only at the block level, which entails a significant number of pages. The erasing process requires the use of a considerable

---

211 Hutchinson, Lee. "Solid-state revolution: in-depth on how SSDs really work." Ars Technica, 6/4/2012. http://arstechnica.com/information-technology/2012/06/inside-the-ssd-revolution-how-solid-state-disks-really-work/

amount of voltage.

A freshly erased, blank page of NAND flash has no charges stored in any of its floating gates. Therefore, as previously stated, the values in storage are all "1s." Changing these values into "0s" entails a dangerous operation requiring the use of high voltages. Consequently, in order to avoid corruption and damage, deleting data on a SSD is done only in increments of entire blocks.[212]

SSD built-in sanitization commands work pretty well in theory, but in practice ...? That's a different story. When these commands are improperly designed or implemented, the erasure techniques will not be effective. However, there is a very simple solution, but is neither pleasant, nor elegant. Yet, it is a 100% effective. I will tell you about it a little bit later...

Any modern cyber system generates a sizeable amount of data marked for disposal and eradication. In a SSD environment, just like in your residential neighborhood, there is a need to organize garbage collection at a predetermined schedule. Enters the SSD garbage collector!

The garbage collection technique on a SSD is designed to maintain the SSD operationally fast and fresh. As pages are modified by being rewritten as new pages, the SSD keeps track of pages with fresh and current data, and those containing data marked for deletion. Since these pages are not individually erasable, the SSD controller will select an opportune moment to perform garbage collection on the pages selected for deletion. The SSD will take an entire block containing both current and erasable pages, will copy the current and fresh pages to a different block, and will erase the entire block selected for garbage collection. Why? Because SSD technology limits the erasing procedure to erase data only at the block level.[213]

_____

212 Ibid
213 Ibid

You may be looking for a 100% effective data sanitization, because the storage device in your cyber system holds very sensitive data, that if recovered by unauthorized hands can seriously jeopardize your enterprise or personal security. Under these conditions, therefore, there is only one possible course of action; the physical destruction of either the HDD or the SSD you are using for data storage. This course of action is the best method to mitigate the risk of data remanence recovery. Since software sanitization techniques offer no guarantees that a 100% of the stored data has been destroyed, a destructive method is preferable, including incineration, pulverization, or any other destruction technique rendering the storage device unusable.[214] There is an enlightening and highly entertaining guide on safe approaches to data sanitization, with sound and current advice applicable to both HDDs and SSDs.[215]

A SSD storage device can read and write at the page level, but cannot erase at the page level. Since the erasing process requires the use of a considerable amount of voltage, in order to avoid corruption and damage, data deletion on a SSD is done only in increments of entire blocks.

There is another dimension of computing where the data remanence issue reaches an even higher degree of criticality, that is, the area of the growing distributed networking technology. With the advent of massive data storage and data analytics, enabled by the High Performance Computing (HPC) technology, researchers are relying more and more on the use of Graphics Processing Units (GPUs), because of their capability in providing an advanced level of performance in highly-parallelized data

214 Conrad, Eric, et al. CISSP Study Guide. Syngress, 2015
215 Kingsley-Hughes, Adrian. "How to securely erase hard drives (HDDs) and solid state drives (SSDs)." ZDNet.com, May 16, 2015.
http://www.zdnet.com/article/how-to-securely-erase-hard-drives-hdds-and-solid-state-drives-ssds/

processing environments. We all know how valuable is the addition of GPUs in highly demanding and intensive computing environments.

The use of GPUs in conjunction with CPUs enables the implementation of an expedited computing environment, facilitating the acceleration for computing tasks covering the fields of engineering, analytics, and scientific applications, among many others. GPU accelerators, since their appearance in 2007, greatly enhance the performance of energy-efficient data centers around the world. GPUs work in conjunction with CPUs by redirecting computing-intensive portions of an application to the GPU, while the CPU continues running the remainder of the code. This cooperative computing environment allow applications to run faster. This concerted processing environment is made possible by the particular architectures of a CPU and a GPU, respectively. The former is designed with a few cores optimized for sequential serial processing, while the latter is designed to provide a massive parallel architecture, aided by thousands of smaller but highly efficient cores, configured for efficient multitasking. Together, CPUs and GPUs provide an accelerated and efficient computing environment.[216]

So, where do the use of GPUs and the issue of data remanence intersect? In the simplest form, the problem resides on the fact that the benefits offered by GPUs are counteracted by the feasibility of memory attacks on GPUs. The expensive predicament of operating an HPC environment requires that the operational costs are distributed among several different clients. Consequently, data remanence from one client may remain in the GPUs memory, thus generating the risk that such memory remanence may become accessible to a subsequent client using the same HPC environment than the previous client.

The risks associated with GPU memory remanence may include the processing of cryptographic keys, sensitive

216 NVIDIA. "WHAT IS GPU ACCELERATED COMPUTING?" NVIDIA.com, 2016. http://www.nvidia.com/object/what-is-gpu-computing.html

private network traffic, or financial data. In a multi-user environment, malicious actors may engage in password discovery, network topology information, and malware concealment. When a subsequent malicious user operates on a multi-user GPU environment, the application processed by this actor may require the allocation of the same memory segment employed by the previous user. Under this scenario, the malicious user can dump the remanent data stored in the shared GPU memory. These are only some scenarios raising the issue of data remanence security risks.[217]

As we can gather from this cursory review, data remanence is an issue that deserves serious attention, that is, if you care for the confidentiality of your data, at either the personal or enterprise level. Data remanence in the context of HDD storage is a matter that requires attention, but the risk is easily mitigated by implementing the many available solutions and guides offered for HDD users. The problem of data remanence reaches a higher degree of criticality for SSD users. There are very few guides offering mitigation techniques, but the main issue resides in the fact that the few tools available to the SSD user are either inadequately implemented, or are simply unreliable.

Data remanence in the context of SSD storage devices represents an extremely serious problem. If the user is a private individual that is left to wrestle with this issue on his own, such user may mitigate the risk by keeping the SSD storage device earmarked for disposal under his strict control. If, on the other hand, there is a corporate user who is storing data on a multi-user environment, such user has no control on the storage device, and no control on mitigating or solving the data remanence risk, either at the drive level or at the memory level.

The reader belonging to the category of multi-user will do

---

217 Bellekens, Xavier. "Data Remanence and Digital Forensic Investigation for CUDA Graphics Processing Units." pure.strath.ac.uk, May, 2015. https://pure.strath.ac.uk/portal/files/42870176/Bellekens_etal_DISSECT201 5_data_remanence_digital_forensic_investigation_CUDA.pdf.

well in assessing and incorporating this risk into his disaster recovery plan. Data submitted for SSD storage in a multi-user environment offers no concrete or acceptable solution to the user, simply because such user does not own the SSD storage media, and it cannot exercise any control to verify that data sanitization is done properly.

So we come to the crucial point where we need to ask ourselves: is there a reliable procedure to ensure data sanitization on SSD media can be effectively accomplished? Subsequently, we need to prepare ourselves to ask the following question: if there is such a reliable procedure, is it available to my data set, scheduled for sanitization?

As we have already mentioned before in this chapter, SSD storage media has available built-in sanitization commands that are effective, if and when implemented correctly. However, there is no guarantee that all manufacturers implement them incorrectly. When we use the term "sanitization" we envision a process designed to render a data set hosted on a SSD storage device completely unavailable and impossible to recover. However, the very technological complexity of SSD storage media becomes one of the main obstacles in achieving effective sanitization.[218]

Data remanence from one client may remain in the GPUs memory, thus generating the risk that such memory remanence may become accessible to a subsequent client using the same HPC environment than the previous client.

Let's remember what we already covered in this chapter: The performance gain we achieve with SSD storage place us in the position where the SSD storage device creates multiple copies of data that are rendered practically invisible to the average user, but discoverable and recoverable to a

---

218 Wei, Michael, et al. "Reliably Erasing Data From Flash-Based Solid State Drives." 2011.
https://www.usenix.org/legacy/event/fast11/tech/full_papers/Wei.pdf

third party with the cyber skills and tools to perform the recovery. Therefore, any regular SSD user, lacking specialized knowledge and tools to obtain information on residual copies of data, is unable to determine when data sanitization is properly implemented on the SSD storage device.

The bad news: data may remain on the SSD storage device after the original user decides to dispose of it. The problem? That data is discoverable and recoverable, and once extracted by a third party, may exposed sensitive or confidential information. Since there is no reliable solution provided by built-in software commands, the SSD user should be prepared to apply the only guaranteed solution to the data remanence problem; total physical destruction of the SSD storage device.

The user should be aware that the SSD storage device is basically a collection of NAND memory cells, and each one of these cells should be destroyed. Thus, a single destructive blow to the SSD device may not be sufficient, since some of the memory cells may remain intact after the single destructive impact. The user should dismantle the SSD device, and ensure that every memory cell is irrecoverably destroyed. That is, if the user wants to assume the responsibility of ensuring the destruction of the memory cells is irreversible. Does a regular user have the equipment necessary to ensure irreversible physical destruction of the memory cells?

Some commercial vendors dedicated to the physical destruction of SSDs recommend the use of their services, by physically shredding the memory cells in their industrial facilities, or an alternative method of a cruncher at a user's location. This latter solution offers the user full control of their data destruction process, plus an auditing program to create a record of all destroyed SSD media.[219]

The performance gain we achieve with SSD

219 Verity Systems. "How do you destroy SSD?" Verysystems.com, March 9, 2016. http://www.veritysystems.com/news-blog/how-do-you-destroy-ssd/

storage place us in the position where the SSD storage device creates multiple copies of data that are rendered practically invisible to the average user, but discoverable and recoverable to a third party with the cyber skills and tools to perform the recovery.

Some of these vendors provide very specific information regarding a protocol required to achieve the desired goal of irreversible physical destruction of SSD memory cells. They sponsore industrial shredding as the best practice, but they emphasize the importance of achieving the optimum particle size during the shredding process. They advise that the standard one-inch particle size configured on standard industrial shredders is ineffective when shredding SSD memory cells. That one-inch size configuration will allow the small memory cells to slip through the hammers in the shredder, thus leaving sensitive information intact. They discovered that the optimum particle size configuration on the shredder should be set to half an inch, or smaller; this is critical to ensure the success on obliterating the small memory cells, thus eliminating the risk of data remanence.[220]

Of course, the final decision as to what method and protocol for data destruction on SSD media remains the prerogative of the user. However, I remind the user seeking for a SSD data destruction solution to seriously consider the critical chain of evidence protocol. If the data you manage, either at the personal or enterprise scope, reside at a level of confidentiality or sensitivity requiring a strict control, then the management protocol must be based on tracking and auditing the status of each decommissioned SSD storage device, maintaining an indisputable inventory record for each destroyed SSD device. At the personal level, this strict control will provide the user with peace of mind. At the enterprise level, it will provide a significant reduction on liability risks.

---

220 Securis. "Destroying Solid State Drives– Size Does Matter." Securis.com, Oct 29th, 2012. http://www.securis.com/destroying-solid-state-drives-size-does-matter/

Blank page for the reader's personal notes

Chapter 15. Unintended Cyber Path

As we approach the last part of this book, I consider necessary to focus on reflecting on one of the most prevailing cyber threats, the one that transcends all precautions and technical defenses; the human factor

Every network, public or private, is accessible by agents with the require knowledge, expertise, and motivation. The bottom line: there is no defense against human gullibility, always present, always active. Besides, we entrust the protection of our networks to system administrators, but the authority to make, or dismiss any cyber security measure is decided by managers and supervisors, most of the time selected because of their political influence, not because of their cyber technical expertise. These managers and supervisors, in turn, are susceptible to the follies of human gullibility, or in some other cases, exhibiting both gullibility and apathy toward cyber security, and arrogance. Sometimes they even succumb to a psychological reversal by seeing themselves not as public servants, serving an organization and a mission they have been tasked to protect. Rather, they digress into seeing themselves as the rulers of their own feud, answerable to nobody but themselves.

The principles of cyber security are constantly in conflict with the demands of convenience and ease of use. The clamor of the majority is always for "we want it now, we want it simple, and we want it easy." Because of this demands there are numerous violations against the fundamentals principles of cyber security. If the reader would like to be reminded of a recent illustration on the disastrous results of these violations we don't have to look any further than the national security disaster caused by the flagrant disregard for the tenets of cyber security; the OPM data breach

Before we launch into considering the factors leading to this breach disaster, we should also consider the premises behind this disaster. The OPM is a government agency tasked with the responsibility of collecting, processing, and guarding very sensitive information of a very private nature regarding individuals performing a service for the USA, and requiring a security clearance.

Thus, the responsibility of the senior leaders on this agency is commensurate to the important task of the agency they serve. Their task in leading this agency is explicitly and intimately related to the national security of the US government. That is to say their task and responsibility is neither a trivial nor an inconsequential one. Errors in judgment at their level of leadership carry severe and non-linear consequences, escalating into exponential levels of complexity, with severe damage inflicted on US national security.

Other data breaches in the US affecting our nation during the period 2014-2017 include the Postal Service, the State Department (reported March 2015), the Nuclear Regulatory Commission, the IRS (spanning between January 2014 and March 2015, and reported January 2016), and the White House. However, none of these data breaches reaches the critical and massive harm inflicted upon our national security as the OPM data breach, publicly acknowledged in June 2015.[221]

We entrust the protection of our networks to system administrators, but the authority to make, or dismiss any cyber security measure is decided by managers and supervisors, most of the time selected because of their political influence, not because of their cyber technical expertise.

The stolen data affects over 22 millions of former and current

---

221 Majority Staff Report, Committee on Oversight and Government Reform US House of Representatives 114th Congress. "The OPM Data Breach: How the Government Jeopardized Our National Security for more than a Generation." Sept 7, 2016. www. oversight.house.gov

government employees, since the extracted data includes security clearance background information on all affected victims. This information contains highly detailed personally identifiable information (PII) on the affected employees, their families, and other contacts. The possession of this PII information in the hands of cyber adversaries renders each one of the affected millions of employees as a potential target for adversarial intelligence agencies.[222]

The cyber intrusion and data extraction was facilitated by the incompetence of OPM leadership in failing to prioritize the criticality of implementing the proper cyber security measures to protect the highly sensitive stolen data. The inveterate cyber security deficiency sustained by OPM had been reported and denounced since 2005 as a cyber weakness condition, and in 2014 the OPM Inspector General upgraded this vulnerability to a "significant deficiency" status. The OPM leadership, nevertheless, failed to implement any corrective actions and establish a secure cyber security posture.

There seems to be a common denominator among some leaders appointed to protect sensitive cyber data; they seem to be completely oblivious to the tenets of cyber security, while maintaining an arrogant attitude of forgetting that they are appointed to serve the people of the United States, and protect the US interests in national security. Instead, they assume they answer to nobody but themselves, and proceed to make decisions leading to the harming of US interests.

I consider it is prudent to examine a contemporary case just prior to examining the OPM data breach, simply because of the presence of the common denominator factor, arrogance, we just mentioned. For instance, there was a former female Secretary of State, who was in office from 2009 to 2013. She stated that her unlawful use of a private email server didn't include any classified information, and added that the computer server hosting her emails "was in a private building protected by the US Secret Service." She also explained that in her decision to use private email "I opted for

---

222 Ibid

convenience," she concluded.[223] Do these appointed leaders show any comprehension on the tenets of cyber security? Obviously not, because in the case of this former Secretary of State she doesn't know that walls and guns do not protect against a cyber intrusion! Her ignorance and disregard for the principles of cyber security is simply deplorable!

The FBI conducted an investigation on the matter of these private servers used by this former Secretary. The investigation shows that during her tenure at the State Department she used severals private email servers and server administrators, along with numerous mobile devices associated and connected to that personal domain. As new servers were implemented, the older ones were decommissioned and stored in various ways,[224] though not necessarily in accordance with cyber security principles.

For instance, when one of the original personal servers was decommissioned in 2013, only the email software was removed, while leaving the email data intact. Among the thousands of emails the FBI found there were three classified, one at the Secret level and two at the Confidential level, as of the time when they were sent or received.[225]

In response to the FBI investigation, the attorneys of the former Secretary conducted a search on the personal email server. The attorneys conducted the search by focusing only on the emails header information, not on the body of the emails. In doing so they were attempting to determine which ones they considered to be work-related emails from more than 60,000 emails remaining on the former Secretary's personal system in 2014. As result of these searches, her

223 Perez. E., & Prokupecz, S. "Sources: State Dept. hack the 'worst ever'." CNN, March 10, 2015, http://www.cnn.com/2015/03/10/politics/state-department-hack-worst-ever/index.html
224 Comey, James. "Statement by FBI Director James B. Comey on the Investigation of Secretary Hillary Clinton's Use of a Personal E-Mail System." FBI National Press Office, July 5, 2016. https://www.fbi.gov/news/pressrel/press-releases/statement-by-fbi-director-james-b-comey-on-the-investigation-of-secretary-hillary-clinton2019s-use-of-a-personal-e-mail-system
225 Ibid

attorneys provided approximately 30,000 emails to the State Department in December 2014. Among these, 110 emails contained classified information at the time they were sent or received. Eight of the email chains contained information at the Top Secret level at the time they were sent. Subsequently, the former Secretary's attorneys deleted all the remaining emails they deemed not to be work-related, and then they cleaned and purged the email systems in such a way as to prevent any further forensic recovery of the email data.[226]

In his official public statement, the FBI Director stated that there is evidence that the former Secretary and her colleagues "were extremely careless in their handling of very sensitive, highly classified information."[227] There were seven email chains with data classified at the Top Secret/Special Access Program level when they were sent and received. Both the sending and receiving parties should have known that an unclassified system was not the proper media for exchanging and storing that level of classified data, since "all these emails were housed on unclassified personal servers not even supported by full-time security staff." The FBI investigation found evidence that "the security culture of the State Department in general, and with respect to use of unclassified e-mail systems in particular, was generally lacking in the kind of care for classified information found elsewhere in the government."[228]

With regard to the possibility of cyber intrusion by foreign adversaries into the former Secretary's personal email system, the FBI assesses that hostile actors did gained access to the private commercial email accounts of people in regular contact with the former Secretary's personal account. Additionally, she continued using her personal email extensively while outside the United States, including work-related email correspondence while in the territory of advanced cyber adversaries. Considering these combination of factors, the FBI assesses that hostile cyber actors

---

226 Ibid
227 Ibid
228 Ibid

possibly gained access to the former Secretary's personal email account.[229] Allow me to reiterate this once again: her ignorance and disregard for the principles of cyber security and classified material protection are irresponsibly deplorable! After all, a recent press article[230] reminds us that this former Secretary of State was depicted as an insider threat in a cyber security training presentation for soldiers.

This book is all about the cyber path, that wide digital avenue that connects every cyber system in our planet. And in this environment there is always a way to find a path leading to a potential target system. Physical walls and doors, and weapons, do not constitute a deterrent or an obstacle to find the desire target. The path leading to it is digital, and this path can always be intercepted by digital means.

The ignorance exhibited in the statement of that former Secretary of State is abysmal. Was there any cyber security person available to advice her on the appropriate cyber security measures to protect the mail server? I am certain the answer is that there were several qualified cyber experts who tried to do so, but their advice went into deaf ears. The worst combination occurs when ignorance is mixed with arrogance. I have encountered many persons in position of authority who erroneously believe that authority spontaneously begets knowledge and wisdom in all matters, and they feel compelled to ignore the advice of experts, because they feel threatened by the true empirical knowledge of such experts.

I have also had the rare privilege of encountering a few leaders who honor and dignify their position of authority by relying on the knowledge and advice of the experts made available to them, and trust and support their expert advice. This kind of leadership is rare, and certainly was not present

229 Ibid
230 Scarborough, Rowan. "U.S. Army depicted Hillary Clinton as insider threat in cyber security training." The Washington Times, February 15, 2017. http://www.washingtontimes.com/news/2017/feb/15/army-depicted-hillary-clinton-insider-threat-cyber/

on the two organizational cases referenced in this chapter.

When exploring these type of cases we realize we are stuck on a vicious cycle of reactionary measures, instead of embarking on an anticipatory and precautionary plan on cyber security. I wonder what Santayana would think of the type of American leaders who love to pay lip service to the maxim he coined, without ever practicing the tenets implied in that maxim.[231]

Physical walls and doors, and weapons, do not constitute a deterrent or an obstacle to find the desire cyber target. The path leading to it is digital, and this path can always be intercepted by digital means.

The cyber intrusions deeply affecting us during this last decade are a perfect illustration for this aphorism. Case after case we continue to repeat the same mistake of entrusting the cyber security of invaluable and highly sensitive data to individuals exercising their authority without the proper knowledge and counsel, and repeating the same costly mistakes of others. The saddest part of it all is that such costly mistakes have all been repeated during the same decade. Is it that hard to remember the past mistakes during a single decade?!

Furthermore, these are not just mistakes; these cyber intrusions are the result of flagrant and willful violations of US government policies and protocols, committed personally by those who were entrusted to protect such sensitive data. Perhaps many readers may recall the 1997 book popularizing the "dereliction of duty" terminology, that as a legal offense is still quite relevant today. Why bringing this topic in relation to the unlawful use of personal email servers and the OPM data breach cases? Because a common denominator, namely, human arrogance, is present in all

---

231 George Santayana, the philosopher who coined the aphorism "Those who cannot remember the past are condemned to repeat it." Santayana, George, 1905, Reason in Common Sense, p. 284, volume 1 of The Life of Reason

contributing factors in the behavior of all three appointed leaders involved in the State Department and the OPM cases. Thus, dereliction of duty applies to the unlawful use of personal email servers and the OPM data breach. Why? Because in both cases we have a failure by organization leaders to abide by the standing rules of the constitution or by-laws of the organization they were appointed to serve, or a failure to perform the duties of the position to which these irresponsible leaders were appointed.[232]

A recent article points to 2014 as the year of the breach, considering that as many as 10 government agencies were reported as experiencing cyber intrusions.[233] In the majority of these cases a recurrent smoke screen was used to attempt deflecting the responsibility from those entrusted with protecting sensitive data but failed to do so. The smoke screen systematically used the cliché of characterizing the cyber intrusion as "very sophisticated." This repetitive claim would have some degree of validity if the organizations victimized by the data breach would had had a robust cyber security posture. The well known fact is they did not have such robust cyber security. Therefore, the mantra "very sophisticated" is a smoke screen designed to implied there was no possible defense against the cyber attack, and to deflect the responsibility from those gullible and irresponsible individuals who fell for such trivial cyber attack. Let's just ask one very simple question: how many of the cyber attacks included a preliminary spear phishing attack? Is spear phishing a "very sophisticated" attack? No, it is a very simple and low tech attack.

Let us now return to the OPM data breach case we briefly placed in hiatus. Perhaps a succinct analysis of this infamous breach may give us an even darker and more critical view of the damage caused to national security by the irresponsible behavior and apathy of leaders entrusted with

---

232 US Legal. "Dereliction of Duty Law and Legal Definition."
    https://definitions.uslegal.com/d/dereliction-of-duty/
233 Moore, Jack. "The Year of the Breach: 10 Federal Agency Data Breaches in 2014." NextGov.com, December 30, 2014.
    http://www.nextgov.com/cybersecurity/2014/12/year-breach-10-federal-agency-data-breaches-2014/102066/

the protection of sensitive PII. Their failure to protect this data has placed everyone holding a US government clearance into a vulnerable existence, because their personal data, and that of their relatives and acquaintances is in the hands of US adversaries and cyber criminals.

As accurately described in an insightful paper,[234] the OPM data breach can be described as the result of "a cascading failure of controls" leading to that national security disaster, brought in front of the national conscience not by the OPM leadership, but by an article in the press in July 2014.[235] This article reported the March breach into the OPM database. Spokespersons from the affected agency stated at the time of the article that no PII was compromised, though this statement was misleadingly incorrect. The same press article also pointed out that the previous year the Department of Energy suffered the loss of PII as well.

The mantra "very sophisticated" is a smoke screen designed to implied there was no possible defense against the cyber attack, and to deflect the responsibility from those gullible and irresponsible individuals who fell for such trivial cyber attack.

The cyber security posture of OPM prior to the data breach was deplorable. Should OPM have implemented the Critical Security Control 17 (CSC 17) regarding data protection, the data breach could have been prevented or, at the very least, minimized. Should OPM have implemented CSC 17-1, the policy of encryption for sensitive data at rest, this encryption would have rendered the compromise considerably less

234 Belangia, David. "That's where the Data is! Why Break into the Office of Personnel Management Systems – Because That Is Where the Sensitive Information for Important People Is Maintained!" SANS Institute, 2014-11-03. https://www.sans.org/reading-room/whitepapers/bestprac/data-is-break-office-personnel-management-systems-35577

235 Schmidt, Sanger and Perlroth. "Chinese Hackers Pursue Key Data on U.S. Workers." New York Times, July 9, 2014. https://www.nytimes.com/2014/07/10/world/asia/chinese-hackers-pursue-key-data-on-us-workers.html?_r=0

damaging, by negating the cyber intruder the ability to quickly using the stolen data.[236]

The same insightful paper points out that both Oracle and Microsoft employ the Transport Data Encryption (TDE) technology. This is a file level encryption that greatly enhances the level of protection to data at rest, by encrypting the information on the hard drive, and ensuring the backed up data is also encrypted. Why was this technology not implemented on the OPM network?

And then, what about when this sensitive data is not at rest, but rather in motion? The implementation of CSC 17-7, encryption for data in motion, would have provided a robust cyber protection. At the OPM, the E-QIP system is a web based interface to a database. The Transport Layer Security (TLS), designed to provide with end-to-end encryption during traffic, regardless of the route followed by the data in transit, comes into play. Implementing TLS provides confidentiality and integrity for data in motion, between the requester and the server. Additionally, with the deprecation of SHA-1 and its replacement with SHA-2 algorithm, encrypting data in motion will ensure additional protection for critical data. The implementation of encryption for data in motion ensures additional protection for sensitive critical information.[237]

To truly assess the grave harm done to the US national security, as a result of the disastrous OPM data breach, we need to explore the findings disclosed in the official government report resulting from the investigation on this tragic event. This report was delivered to the public in September 2016.[238]

The OPM data breached resulted in the data theft of the

236 Belangia
237 Ibid
238 Committee on Oversight and Government Reform U.S. House of Representatives, 114th Congress. "The OPM Data Breach: How the Government Jeopardized Our National Security for More than a Generation." September 7, 2016. https://oversight.house.gov/wp-content/uploads/2016/09/The-OPM-Data-Breach-How-the-Government-Jeopardized-Our-National-Security-for-More-than-a-Generation.pdf

security clearance background investigation data. This type of data, belonging to more than 22 million individuals, was compromised, causing critical and irreversible damage to our national security, and to the personal security of the affected individuals as well. The report states that despite the high value data OPM was instructed to protect, this "agency failed to prioritize cyber security [to] secure [this] high value data."[239] The OPM Inspector General (OIG) had warned this agency regarding its cyber vulnerabilities since 2005, and in 2014 OPM was declared to have a significant deficiency, due to the "absence of an effective managerial structure to implement reliable IT security policies." The OPM's compromised IT systems were operating without a security assessment and valid Authority to Operate (ATO). Specifically, the Personnel Investigations Processing System, the Enterprise Server Infrastructure, and the LAN/WAN "were all operating on expired Authorities to Operate at the time of the data breach."[240]

On March 20, 2014 OPM received another warning from the Department of Homeland Security's Computer Emergency Response Team (US_CERT). The warning indicated that unauthorized data extraction was taking place on the OPM network. However, OPM senior leadership failed to heed this warning, thus allowing the intruders to extract sensitive data providing a road map to the OPM cyber environment, thus facilitating the impending data breach. Specifically, the extracted data contained manuals about the servers and OPM network environment, thus providing the intruders with valuable information about the OPM network infrastructure.

US-CERT stated that OPM IT leadership circumvented existing security policies in order to execute business functions, thus "exposing the entire agency to unnecessary risk."[241] This proves that the OPM data breach was foreseen, predicted, and documented, prior to the November 2015 officially reported data breach. On May 2014 an intruder established a successful foothold into OPM cyber

---

239 Ibid
240 Ibid
241 Ibid

environment, installed malware, and create a backdoor to access OPM network, while remaining undetected. This intruder then proceeded to extract security clearance sensitive data, beginning in July 2014. This unlawful data extraction was preventable, provided the OPM senior leadership would have implemented the available cyber security countermeasures required to stop the adversarial data theft.

The two OPM leaders, namely the Director and the CIO, concealed the OPM data breach when testifying before the Committee on Oversight and Government Reform. During this June 2014 occasion they omitted in their testimony that OPM had experienced a significant data breach in March 2014. An event of this magnitude is reportable by law, but the Director and CIO did not reported the incident. The revelation on the OPM data breach was brought before the public eye by a press article,[242] explaining the severe implications of the stolen data.

The OPM data breached resulted in the theft of the security clearance background investigation data belonging to more than 22 million individuals, causing critical and irreversible damage to our national security, and to the personal security of the affected individuals as well.

There was a persistent practice on the part of both the Director and the CIO in the OPM case. They sought to obfuscate the truth regarding the intrusion details, such as in the case of misleading testimonies regarding the incident response and forensic support role provided by a contractor. Archuleta and Seymour denied the fact that the contractors detected the intrusion, and instead declared that OPM had done so. Subsequently, OPM deleted the forensic data collected by the contractor on the OPM network, showing the extent and severity of the cyber intrusion. When OPM deleted the data collected by the contractor, OPM acted in

---

242 Schmidt, Sanger and Perlroth.

violation of their obligation to preserve this evidence relevant to the Committee's investigation, acting against the data preservation order issued by the Committee. The order was issued on August 21, 2015, and the OPM deletion was conducted between August 17 and 19, 2015.[243]

The US House Oversight & Government Reform Committee report explicitly states that as of September 2016 the details of the cyber intrusion remain unclear, "due to sloppy cyber hygiene and inadequate security technologies" prevailing in the OPM cyber environment.[244] Furthermore, OPM destroyed forensic evidence (more than 11,000 files) gathered by a forensic service contractor, and OPM leadership downplayed the true impact of the data breach, even to the point of the former OPM CIO Donna Seymour making "a series of false and misleading statements under oath regarding the agency's response" to the cyber intrusions.[245]

This former CIO went as far as to omit the theft of documents during the hearing before the Senate Homeland Security in June 2014. Former OPM Director Archuleta also made questionable statements under oath regarding the cyber intrusion incidents. Both the former OPM Director and the former OPM CIO "engaged in activities that hindered the work of the OIG."[246]

Furthermore, there were serious concerns raised by the OIG and Congress regarding Seymour's fitness to serve as CIO, but she was allowed to remain in her appointed position. Chairman Chaffetz stated in a letter to Acting Director Cobert that he had lost his confidence in Seymour, and keeping her in place only added "insult to injury" to those whose sensitive PII was stolen. Cobert did not remove Seymour, but gave her a vote of confidence instead.[247]

---

243 Committee on Oversight and Government Reform U.S. House of
    Representatives, 114th Congress.
244 Ibid
245 Ibid
246 Ibid
247 Ibid

The persistent failure of OPM's leadership to implement basic cyber security, despite years of warnings from the Inspector General, and the availability of preventive and defensive cyber tools, can only be attributed to indolence and irresponsibility. The OPM breach is a case of human failure, not a technology failure, since OPM leadership failed to implement the available protective cyber measures. Evidence provided by US-CERT establishes that the cyber intruders had access to OPM network since July 2012, but OPM leadership repeatedly failed to take the appropriate cyber protective measures to defend the highly sensitive data entrusted to them.[248] I believe I already introduced the concept of dereliction of duty just prior to this cursory analysis of the OPM grave and disastrous data breach, facilitated by the irresponsible OPM leaders at the helm of this organization during the time of the cyber intrusion.

This case of unintended path, leading to a severely damaging effect to our national security, is representative of our culture failing to understand the basic principles of cyber security, in conjunction with the political appointment of leaders who lack the knowledge and motivation to implement and enforce the require cyber security measures. In the cyber dimension there is one predominant principle; the in-depth knowledge of the cyber dimension is paramount, and only qualified cyber experts should be in charged of agencies charged with the protection of highly sensitive data. Political appointees are a necessary evil in our society, but they should not have the final word when confronting a cyber adversary. Only the qualified cyber experts, not pretenders, should be in charge of facing cyber adversaries and protecting our valuable sensitive data.

This case of unintended path shows not only the ignorance, but also the willful decision of the OPM leaders to conceal information during the investigation, and to misinform and deny the facts surrounding this damaging data breach. They hosted and facilitated for a long period of time the unknown and undetected presence of the intruders, siphoning sensitive data, and when they finally were confronted with

---

248 Ibid

the facts of the intrusions, they opted to conceal it and deny it, in order to protect their own personal interests. Is that the kind of honorable code required of our civil servant leaders?

There is a reputable cyber security analyst who states that the timeline of major events in the OPM data breach highlights the series of miscalculations incurred by the OPM senior leadership, portraying their willful underestimation of the gravity of the threat targeting their agency.[249]

I am positively sure that in the minds of the two irresponsible OPM leaders who facilitated this disastrous data breach, they are convincing themselves that they didn't mean to cause this harm. After all, this is one of the earliest cope out mechanism we all learn at a very early age, when we discover that we can always deflect responsibility from our acts when we proclaim: "I didn't mean to ..."

Oh yes, that amazingly effective way of saying: "don't hold me responsible for what I did, because I didn't mean to ..." Against all logic, such cope out mechanism still works, and shields us from assuming responsibility for whatever damaging behavior, or activity conducing to harm, from which we want to be excused. Let us examine this cope out statement from a logical and psychological point of view.

With the "I didn't mean to ..." statement we are pursuing a double goal: to convince ourselves, and those affected for our damaging behavior and actions, that there is no meaning associated with such behavior and actions. This is clearly a deceptive strategy; saying we didn't mean it "is a way of dodging the bullet."[250] A gifted psychotherapist raises the incisive question: if we claim that we didn't mean what we did or said, who did?[251] The alternative of claiming that we did or say something that we didn't mean to do or say leads

249 Krebs. "Congressional Report Slams OPM on Data Breach." Krebs on Security, Sep 7, 2016. https://krebsonsecurity.com/tag/opm-breach/
250 Mathews, Andrea. 'I Didn't Mean It,' or 'It Didn't Mean Anything.' Psychology Today, Feb 01, 2015. https://www.psychologytoday.com/blog/traversing-the-inner-terrain/201502/i-didnt-mean-it-or-it-didnt-mean-anything
251 Ibid

us to a very disturbing conclusion: we are not in control of our thoughts or actions, and this condition becomes a factor that automatically disqualifies an individual in a position of leadership; a leader must remain in control of what she does and says.

The unintended path followed by the highly sensitive PII stolen data from the OPM cyber systems is inexcusable. Perhaps a child or an adolescent may still play the game of "I didn't mean to ..." occasionally, but appointed leaders tasked to safeguard the safety and integrity of sensitive data are not allowed to play this game. A responsible leader charged with such important task should manifest the honorable demeanor where every single behavior or word has meaning, whereby such leader has a clear and specific intention supporting what he/she does or say.[252]

This unintended path led to facilitate the unlawful activity of the foreign power who took advantage of the appallingly deficient and missing cyber security measures and procedures, the ones that Archuleta and Seymour willfully fail to implement, even after repeated cyber security warnings issued to them on multiple occasions. Should they pretend that the unintended path was the result of non-deliberate or unintentional circumstances, then they are admitting failure to discharge their official duty. The unintended path leading to the theft of very sensitive PII is the result of incompetence and willful apathy, causing a grave harm to US interests and national security, and placing at risk over 22 millions of individuals who are, ever since the data breach, and will remain, a potential target for the foreign powers now in possession of the stolen sensitive data.

The OPM breach is a case of human failure, not a technology failure, since OPM failed to implement the available protective cyber measures.

I am also certain that several astute readers have already

---

252 Ibid

notice my lack of emphasis on discussing attribution for this gravest OPM data breach. My answer: Why should I jump in the band wagon of attribution when every media outlet and commentator have already done so? The real issue with the OPM data breach is not who did it, but rather who failed to prevent it! The US as a nation will always be targeted by our adversaries, who will go after collecting our nation's sensitive data, in order to obtain a tactical and strategic advantage over the US. In spending so much time and energy in pinpointing attribution, we are actually following a path of distraction; we are failing to focus on the root cause.

The root cause is the inadequacy, the insufficient and deplorable state of lack of cyber security endemically weakening the cyber security posture of the OPM network. How do we know that such deplorable conditions have been corrected, and the proper cyber security measures have been implemented? How do we know that OPM network personnel have implemented the required policies and countermeasures to face subsequent cyber attacks? How do we know that OPM has implemented the required procedures to overcome the network security shortcomings leading to the data breach? How do we know that OPM has hired the qualified cyber security personnel required to maintain and enhance a strong network security posture? How do we know that OPM has actually implemented a professional team dedicated to enforce the intrusion prevention strategies and policies that were lacking prior to the cyber intrusion? How do we know, factually, that the cyber intruders have actually been neutralized?

And more important of all, how do we know that OPM is now under the leadership of qualified professionals who actually know how to protect the OPM network? Because if OPM is now under the leadership of alternative political appointees with a degree of cyber incognizance similar to that of Archuleta and Seymour, then we are simply waiting for the next great data theft episode. This is a good place to remind ourselves of Santayana's maxim quoted earlier in this chapter. The answers to these questions constitute the core of the things that are important to know. When we know, promote, enhance, and enforce the proper cyber security measures, then we become capable of defending the OPM's sensitive data, regardless of the attribution of the adversary targeting this data.

The real issue with the OPM data breach is not who did it, but rather who failed to prevent it!

The unintended path is the unavoidable route that cyber data may transit when exposed to unplanned or unforeseen circumstances resulting from the non-linear series of events affecting the said cyber data. Factors conducive to these circumstances may emerge from a variety of reasons: pre-existing factors unknown to the data owner, lack of cyber security monitoring and controlling, ineptitude, ignorance, or simply contemptuous and willful disregard for cyber security controls. This latter is the genesis of the OPM data breach, leading to the facilitating of the data theft that threatens national security and the well being of over 22 millions of individuals with a US security clearance.

Epilogue

And after all the different paths we have explored in the pages of this book, there is a pending question, ruminating over the possibility that perhaps we might have, inadvertently, overlooked a certain path. This overlooked path, while maintaining the overall goal of targeting victims, in itself is neither completely digital, nor is the final task aiming at harming or modifying a cyber system or its corresponding binary code. Rather, the final task is a much more ethereal and highly complex system; the human brain.

What do we do when we are confronted with a cyber threat that travels a variety of paths, while seeking as its primary and ultimate goal not a cyber system, but rather the mind and behavior of human beings? Is this really a case of a malicious cyber path? Most definitely. Yet, is this really a cyber path departing from the intended and original path?

The answer to this depends on the analysis of this particular phenomenon, that is neither contemporary to the age of the digital computer, nor to the Internet or to the WWW, but rather a late comer threat, gaining its most powerful momentum from the global explosion of social media. The target of this cyber threat is the human mind, and the intent is to influence the actions and behavior of human beings sharing a particular social milieu. This late comer threat has become known as "cognitive hacking." The intent, regardless of the series of events leading to the disclosure of the final attack, is to influence human perceptions, through misinformation, relying on the almost instantaneous dissemination of uncorroborated information through social media peers.

Perhaps one of the most notorious cases of this malicious misinformation campaigns, or cognitive hacking, occurred in August 2000, and may be considered as the antecedent of cognitive hacking. This is the case of the server and storage provider Emulex, targeted by misinformation, resulting on a lost of $2.2 billions in market trades. This was an act of vengeance planned and executed by a 23-year-old hacker, who disseminated fabricated news, misleading investors into believing that Emulex was under the scrutiny of the US Securities and Exchange Commission, a SEC investigation.[253] The hacker created a false press release to cause a drop in the Emulex stock prices, in order to recover his personal loss of $100,000 suffered in a stock short sale. Several major news organizations collected and disseminated this false report without verification.

Though this particular case precedes the explosion of the so-called social media, the media dissemination during 2000 was fast enough to cause the tremendous financial loss suffered by Emulex. However, the main principle is clearly illustrated, and proven, by disseminating misinformation to influence the actions and behavior of investors.

The damage inflicted upon Emulex by this vindictive hacker was not launched by using advanced cyber techniques to penetrate network infrastructures, modifying or corrupting binary code, compromising routers and firewalls, or injecting malware into the enterprise network environment. This hacker simply targeted human perception by delivering false news, creating an altered sense of reality, and manipulating investors into a behavior resulting in billions of dollars of loss for Emulex. His main attack vector? A credible press release containing misinformation. This constitutes the essence of cognitive hacking; the manipulation of human perceptions. A very ethereal attack vector, but tremendously effective, with devastating effects.

While the use of misinformation in human history is not a new technique for controlling perception and human behavior, cognitive hacking is becoming an increasingly unsettling threat because of the force multiplier factor of social media, with its pervasive presence and usually uncontested appearance of credibility, while depending on the absence of independent corroboration, aided by the

---

253 Cibenko, George, et al. "Cognitive Hacking: A Battle for the Mind." IEEE, August 2002. http://www.ists.dartmouth.edu/library/6.pdf

natural gullibility of our human nature.

When it comes to judge the veracity of information during a face-to-face interaction there are several indicators that might aid the recipient of the information into forming an educated assessment regarding the veracity of the received information. Knowledge of the personality, character, and ethical standing of the individual passing the information can prove an invaluable tool for evaluating the credibility of the message. By contrast, social media and other web-based communications establish several degrees of separation between the messenger and the recipients.

While the use of misinformation in human history is not a new technique for controlling perception and human behavior, cognitive hacking is becoming an increasingly unsettling threat because of the force multiplier factor of social media, with its pervasive presence and usually uncontested appearance of credibility.

A very, very long time ago, when there was a degree of credibility associated with honest journalists committed to a code of ethics in disseminating news in an objective manner, we could ascribe some degree of credence to the news and the press. Today, however, journalists no longer maintain these ethical standings, and their message offers a rather transparent view of their personal and/or organizational bias. Thus, the recipient is confined to assess a message that stands on several degrees of separation from the recipient.

When compared to the other technical cyber path threats explored in this book, the cognitive hack path is perhaps the most unsettling, because in many cases there are no clearly defined and objective technical cyber indicators to assist us in detecting the presence of this threat. This contrast hopefully will motivate the reader into attempting a better grasp of the concrete indicators of a technical cyber malicious paths, since they are more objectively identifiable.

The cognitive attack targets the perception of reality shared by a group of human beings, and misleads them into an erroneous course of action. This most insidious cognitive attack introduces a new layer of complexity into the detection of the attack. The new layer of complexity requires new resources that may or may not be available to any particular individual. The effectiveness of disinformation is the difficulty associated with the detection of the falsehood element contained in the disseminated misinformation.

The complexity associated with achieving a certain degree of success in scrutinizing and evaluating the content of the misinformation depends not on a single individual, but on a collective assessment of the disinformation. Thus, if a single individual doesn't possess enough corroborating facts to asses the potential corrupted message disseminated through a cognitive attack, that individual may fall prey to the cognitive attack. And yet, even a certain group, with a collective assessment of the message in question, cannot guarantee the outcome of their assessment, because the message in question may surpass the collective knowledge of that particular group, and the entire group may fall prey to the cognitive attack as well. The dynamics involved in a cognitive attack are non-linear, just as the dynamics of a purely technical cyber binary attack are non-linear as well.

We face a dual layer of concern when confronted by the realities of purely binary attacks, in conjunction with the additional layer represented by the cognitive attack. The complexity of the non-linear cyber dynamics and the corresponding cyber reality milieu have already been outlined in my previous book,[254] and remain an issue demanding our attention and vigilance. Now, in conjunction with the social dynamics of a cognitive attack, operating in juxtaposition in our social milieu, we are confronted by a multifaceted concern that increases to a higher level. The complexity of the dynamics in a case of cognitive attack are well illustrated by the fact that the Emulex episode mentioned at the opening of this epilogue was indeed disseminated by well-established news services. They

---

254 Giannelli, Lou. Cyber Reality. Xlibris, 2016

assumed the disinformation message was accurate, and proceeded to disseminate it without independent verification.[255] These news services had the collective means to verify the corrupted message, but they failed to do so.

While there are many indicators and mitigation techniques to provide us with a degree of protection against purely binary attacks, as outlined in this book, the question remains: what protection or mitigation do we have against cognitive attacks? The answer to this question remains a developing and evolving issue. Why? Because we are facing a complex issue that touches many aspects of our modern life, mixed with the equally complex reality of speech and communication through the Internet infrastructure, upon which the WWW and social media are built. How much legislation is developing to embrace this complex reality? And since legislators are not prepared to interact with the complexities of the cyber reality, because they are not properly equipped to acquired a mature understanding of the cyber dimension, how many of the current legislative attempts will provide a reliable defense against cognitive attacks?

The Internet infrastructure, and the WWW, have become a powerful means for communication in our modern life, but due to its tremendous power to disseminate information, this infrastructure and the corresponding communication facilitators (WWW, social media) have also become both a perception management and a perception manipulation tool. This modern communication medium now compels the legal system to examine and reexamine fundamental principles regulating communication in society. According to a scholarly article, there is a 1946 legal tool that is being used to deal with cognitive attacks.[256] Of course, any application of legislation tools generates very volatile exchanges, since this new type of attack targets primarily the perception of human beings, misguiding them into behavioral changes resulting in grave harm to finances and reputations.

255 Cibenko, George, et al. "Cognitive Hacking." Oct 2003.
   http://www.ists.dartmouth.edu/library/301.pdf
256 Ibid

This book intends to provide the reader with a map and itinerary to travel the complex cyber dimension. There are so many devices and technologies interacting in the cyber dimension. Some are tangible and visible, while others remain in a background most of the time inaccessible to the regular cyber user. The intent of this book is to enable the reader to exercise a degree of control over the cyber devices that are part of our modern life, while protecting our private interests that may become negatively affected by threats to the plethora of cyber devices surrounding our daily lives. The premise of this book is to remind the reader this axiom: we humans are at the top of the creation order, and we should exercise control over the cyber devices at our disposition.

We should not allow these cyber devices, and their underlying technologies, to control and manipulate our daily lives. We should be in control of them, and protect ourselves from any form of exploitation designed by malicious individuals controlling such devices for their selfish gain.

The cyber path is complex and non-linear. However, any responsible individual committed to protect his or her personal interests, and those of their beloved ones, can certainly exercise a degree of control over cyber devices and cyber technologies, by using reputable information to learn how to achieve a degree of control and protection over them.

Alphabetical Index

www.ingramcontent.com/pod-product-compliance
Lightning Source LLC
Chambersburg PA
CBHW051049050326
40690CB00006B/657